FUTURE FINTECH FRAMEWORK

A Vision to Simplify Understanding, Foster Innovation & Accelerate Growth in Fintech

KARTIK SWAMINATHAN

Notion Press

No. 8, 3rd Cross Street,
CIT Colony, Mylapore,
Chennai, Tamil Nadu – 600 004

First Published by Notion Press 2021
Copyright © Kartik Swaminathan 2021
All Rights Reserved.

ISBN 978-1-63714-723-8

This book has been published with all efforts taken to make the material error-free after the consent of the author. However, the author and the publisher do not assume and hereby disclaim any liability to any party for any loss, damage, or disruption caused by errors or omissions, whether such errors or omissions result from negligence, accident, or any other cause.

While every effort has been made to avoid any mistake or omission, this publication is being sold on the condition and understanding that neither the author nor the publishers or printers would be liable in any manner to any person by reason of any mistake or omission in this publication or for any action taken or omitted to be taken or advice rendered or accepted on the basis of this work. For any defect in printing or binding the publishers will be liable only to replace the defective copy by another copy of this work then available.

DISCLAIMER

This book is an original content, with no content or images (either partially of fully) being taken from any other book, reference material or source. Any resemblance to similar content is purely coincidental and can be based on the fact that the subject Fintech and its constituents are widely discussed, commented and written about. Author has written this book in good faith, so any of the framework, model or approach suggested in the book is purely based on his experience and understanding, and does not constitute any promise or guarantee of any kind.

CONTENTS

Introduction *7*

Who Should Read This Book?. *11*

Section 1 – Key Fintech Themes *15*

This section provides a quick snapshot of some key themes and trends in Fintech. This gets one thinking and ideating with various possibilities for Innovation.

Section 2 – 3F – Future Fintech Framework *49*

A Framework to enable innovation in Fintech, consisting of 3 core components. These 3 components of 3F enable us with a mental map, to create engaging user journeys for various products and solutions, relate technically to a logical architecture and finally, realize the same through a futuristic marketplace.

A.	Fintech Digital Lifecycle (FDLC)	53
B.	Fintech Logical Architecture (FLARE)	89
C.	Fintech API Marketplace (FAM)	102

Section 3 – Other Key Aspects In Fintech 123

Here we discuss certain key aspects, which are important from a business and Fintech ecosystem perspective. Understanding of these key aspects is necessary to Understand, Plan and be prepared for future opportunities.

A. Fintech Players – Current and Emerging 126
B. Changing Income,
   Cost and Pricing Paradigm................137
C. Regulation and Compliance...............144
D. Emergence of New Roles/Career
   Opportunities 156

Going Forward 169

INTRODUCTION

Fintech as the word suggests is the application of Technology to the world of Financial Services, Banking, Investments, Insurance, etc. Over the years, the scope of Fintech has expanded to encompass many aspects like digital, social media, internet, etc., and it has grown in application and size.

Fintech solutions are also increasingly becoming part of our day-to-day lives, and impacting various activities like, making and receiving payments for various purposes like bill payments, purchasing, investing, securing, borrowing, donating, etc. On one hand, we have seen emergence of various solutions like digital wallets, robo advisors, neo banks, payment apps, etc.; on the other hand, Fintech-driven solutions are getting embedded and powering growth in digital commerce or ecommerce as is popularly known. These Fintech solutions have not only added convenience in availing these products and services, but also made the experience more rewarding, not to mention the choices and benefits provided.

All this has happened because of various developments in financial technology, ecosystem and regulations.

However, this evolution is not without any pitfalls and challenges. There is therefore a need to arrange and project this whole ecosystem in a more future-ready framework. So, enter 3F – Future Fintech Framework.

3F or the Future Fintech Framework tries to bring in a very simplified understanding of various aspects driving and impacting Fintech. It then goes on to illustrate how we can assimilate all these aspects into a framework that helps in creating innovative solutions or to make your existing solution better. 3F is technology and product agnostic, and can thereby be applied to most product and solution related use cases in Fintech. In fact, 3F can also be useful and extended to other players in internet space like ecommerce firms, online education, travel, etc.

In simple terms, just like applying the 4P's or the AIDA Model/Framework of marketing helps us to effectively structure and market products, similarly, **3F,** i.e., Future Fintech Framework consists of components which enable in structuring and creating futuristic solutions in the Digital/Fintech space.

This book has 3 key sections:

1. **Key Fintech Themes** – Here we highlight emerging trends and themes that are driving innovation in Fintech.
2. **Future Fintech Framework (3F)** and its 3 main components viz. FDLC, FLARE and FAM.

3. **Other Key Fintech aspects** – Here, we discuss some key aspects like regulations, emerging roles in Fintech, changing players ecosystem and key trends in revenue, pricing and charges.

WHO SHOULD READ THIS BOOK?

This book will **benefit students and professionals** who are either associated with or **wish to make a career in the interesting world of Fintech**. This book provides you with a Framework, enabling you to create a mental map across various aspects of Fintech as below:

a. Understanding various themes or trends in Fintech

b. Innovating and creating new Fintech solutions – FDLC

c. Using a logical structure to understand technology and system, thereby benefitting even non-tech professionals – FLARE

d. How the API Marketplace ecosystem will determine the future course of Fintech – FAM

e. Changing Players Landscape

f. Changing income, cost and pricing paradigms

g. Key aspects pertaining to regulations in Fintech

h. Emerging roles and activities

Now, let us specifically look at how different readers can benefit from the book:

Students (Graduates and above) **across specialization** viz. Management, Engineering, Technology, Commerce, Arts etc. can very quickly get a grasp of the Fintech world. This will help them create a mental map, so they can grasp any new developments in Fintech and understand their linkages, likely impacts, etc. They can also plan their careers and thereby be ready to benefit as career opportunities arise.

Fintech professionals across banks, financial services, payments, lending, insurance, startups, neo banks, eCommerce, blockchain, etc. working in **product management, innovations, digital solutions, marketing, operations, compliance, legal, finance etc.** will get a well-rounded perspective, helping them break silos, and collaborate effectively with others, to build innovative and rewarding solutions for their customers. The way various Fintech aspects have been structured and simplified in the book, it helps bring parity of understanding and appreciation across stakeholders. Templates, requirements, protocols and team structures can be created for better managing new Fintech products/projects. Organizations will thereby experience accelerated innovation and improvement in the success of projects.

Business, Domain and Tech Professionals in IT Firms and Tech startups viz. **sales, pre-sales, solution**

architects, business analysts, developers, etc. can better understand, converse and engage with their customers or stakeholders. 3F also enables them to create innovative prototypes and present use cases more effectively. They can define their solutions user journeys, system requirements and functionality better and also consider various aspects to make the proposition more attractive to the end-user. So, this book will surely improve sales effectiveness, customer engagement and help deliver more meaningful and rounded solutions.

Legal and Compliance professionals related to Fintech will get a better perspective of various aspects and challenges in Fintech and digital space. This in turn will result in better understanding with other stakeholders and effective structuring of solutions from a legal and compliance perspective.

HR Professionals related to Fintech can derive a good understanding from the book thereby enabling them to create suitable roles, Hire effectively, plan training, etc. Not to mention the benefit of better cooperation and collaboration between employees from different departments.

Finally, **the aim of this book is not to share knowledge, but to develop an understanding**, on **how futuristic products/solutions can be structured/created in the Digital/Fintech space**.

Key Fintech Themes

SECTION 01

KEY FINTECH THEMES

Workflow Concierge Societal Automation Assurance Pricing Omnichannel Beyond Convergence Offerings Seamlessness Marketplaces Alliances Microsolutions Web Open Interoperability Chatbots Execution Frauds UX Settlements Alternate Currencies NLU Gamification Data Footprint Disintermediation API customer Analytics Aggregation Multilingual Banking Reconciliation AI Tokenisation Customized Advisory Digital Redemptions time Consortiums Impact Payments 3 Single Identity Interfaces ML Big Wallet Share Profiling Real view P2P Sachetisation Privacy Onboarding 5G Bundling Education Consent Security Loyalty NLP UI Sources Rewards Cloud RPA Solutions Services Connected Emergence Quantum Portability Community Partnership Borders Embedding Platforms IoT Architecture Disputes Differential Based Unbundling Cryptocurrencies Blockchain

There are various key themes or trends that are driving innovation and evolution in the Fintech world. So, before we embark on how we can structure and create a digital product or solution using 3F, under Section 2 of the book, it is important for us to quickly understand these themes or trends in Fintech. This knowledge is especially helpful at the ideation stage, and can be a trigger for new solutions or to improvise existing ones. Many of the themes are business segments in themselves, i.e., with various business models/startups likely to emerge out of each.

Note: For better context and ease of assimilation, we have offered a very quick explanation on each theme/trend, and thereby avoided too much detail. So, given the vastness of many aspects mentioned below, we strongly recommend that you read up further details on these themes through other sources, and deepen your understanding on each, as per your needs. Also, though people with few years of experience may find some of these themes familiar, we suggest that they quickly glance through them, as there may be few more nuggets of information of their interest.

Following are Key Fintech Themes:

i. **Onboarding** – Getting customers onboarded to a Fintech platform quickly is a big theme in Fintech. Challenges exist in terms of documentation, availability of data, compliance, multiple stages of interactions, etc. The aim is to make it easier and quicker to onboard customers and as much through fully digital means. This is where many new Fintech entities are differentiating vis-à-vis incumbents. Availability of APIs, better UI/UX, automation, alternate sources of data, Digital Identity, etc. have fueled different types of onboarding innovations. The benefits are in terms of convenient and quicker onboarding, reduced costs, higher conversion rates, lower dropout rates, improved compliance, improved sales force satisfaction, etc.

ii. **Alternate Data Sources** – The digital environment offers tons of alternate sources of data in form of mobile data, social media, transactions, geolocation, user actions, etc. These are helpful in various ways to better understand the prospects/customer and in turn make specific offerings/products for them. Many Fintech products are tapping into these alternative data sources and offering value adds and enriched experiences to the customers.

iii. **Profiling** – With a wide range of data sources, it has become easier to profile customers based on his demographic segment, preferences, habits, orientation, behavior, influence, etc. Things have gone to the extent where speech/tone analysis, analysis of texting/typing patterns can be used to determine the psychographic profile of customers. All this of course comes with a caveat of privacy norms and what kind of profiling they may or may not allow.

iv. **Digital Footprint and Identity** – Every activity by an individual in the digital medium, be it activity on mobile/website, transactions done, places visited, social connections, etc. can today be tracked. The converse of this is also possible, as people can create digital personas to trick the system. This aspect needs to be kept in mind while developing new solutions. However, this needs to be done in line with relevant regulations.

v. **Analytics** – With all the data available, analytics provide much deeper insight for descriptive, predictive and prescriptive actions. While this is very obvious, in reality, challenges exist in terms of completeness of data, curation of data, storage, understanding interlinkages, linking of data and many more. So, while the science of what to do with data is evolved, the challenge lies with data itself. Also, one needs to think through aspects about data visualization and contextual presentation. As they say, it is good to have clear objectives while working on Analytics Projects, else too much analysis can lead to paralysis.

vi. **Payments** – The payment segment has seen a lot of innovation and improvement within the Fintech space. The key has been convenience, low cost, speed and safety. Innovations in form factors (card, mobile, biometrics, etc.), automation, instant/real time, bill pay, invoicing, travel cards, auto toll collection, different payment types, settlement types, automation in reconciliation, linkage with lending/EMIs, marketing/promotions (promo codes), loyalty, fraud control measures and the list goes on. Newer versions of payment also depend on biometrics, mobile, RFID's, QR codes to move to a cashless and contactless mode (more so for retail-oriented segments). Besides, payment is one segment of Fintech which directly impacts all other segments. Govts and Regulators also realize the larger impact of efficient payment systems, as they can reduce friction in the system and bring efficiencies to overall economic structure.

vii. **Digital Currencies** – Today digital currencies largely exist in forms of cryptocurrencies. However, many governments are mulling issuance of digital currencies, given the rise in Digital Economy. Similarly, we have seen initiatives by social media players to issue their own digital currencies. Another area with activity is cryptocurrencies being used as a medium for global money transfer. However, though the segment is promising, regulators have been cautious. So, need to watch out for developments here.

viii. **Tokenization** – Tokenization implies assigning a unique value to a data, and this helps in security, maintaining anonymity, etc. Tokens are usually generated based on some algorithm and issued on the fly. Tokenization offers benefits during digital processing of transactions. This concept is also used in Blockchain, where tokens are assigned against assets which are transacted/traded.

ix. **Disintermediation** – Traditional business systems consist of a layered distribution structure (Viz. Manufacturers → Distributors → Retailers/Agents → Customers). However, digital solutions offer direct reach to consumers and have disrupted traditional business models. The value propositions offered are in terms of lower cost, faster and better service, etc. We can see disintermediation happening in Fintech too.

x. **Aggregation** – This basically implies aggregating all products and services for customers and bringing it to a single platform. There are stages to this, where it is first within an organization, then across organization and products, segments, etc. Some of this can be enabled through separate entities using APIs. So, be it managing your bank accounts, investments, etc. across different financial entities, aggregation will enable such capabilities and other value adds around it. For e.g., aggregation can help in budgeting and cash-flow analysis, investment/robo advisory, lending, etc.

xi. **Share of wallet** – A mix of effective aggregation and good analytics offer a deeper insight into your engagement with customers, and organizations can get to know their share of customers' wallet. The higher the share of wallet implies better engagement, customer loyalty, referrals and improves profitability. A strong Fintech platform, offering various products, with better features, pricing and engagement is needed for getting a higher share of wallet.

xii. **Single view of customer** – Single view of customer goes beyond aggregation across products. It covers wider aspects including servicing, customer behavior, actions across various channels, etc. The depth of the single view offers a better understanding of customers, to the Sales and Servicing employees. As a perspective, the backend used to create a single view can also evolve into an AI-driven automated offerings/actions engine. Many organizations strive to create Single View of clients and this is also key to offer Omnichannel experience to customers.

xiii. **Advisory and Execution** – In many countries, a very clear split is emerging between Advisory (Recommendation or Advice to buy/sell a particular financial product/service) and Execution (Ability to Transact/Buy/Sell). This may involve new types of certifications/entities and hence, future Fintech platforms will evolve accordingly, keeping such classification in mind.

We may have solutions with Automated Advisory and Execution, as we have seen somewhat with Robo Advisors, algo based trading engines, etc.

xiv. **Education** – Education and Awareness of the customers, employees and agents are a must, especially given the possibility of mis-selling of financial products, frauds and security challenges in Fintech. Currently, this is mandated by regulations in many countries at various levels, but implementation is only largely followed at the employee/agent level, where certifications have been made mandatory. At the customer level, some awareness drives and communication guidelines have been mandated and followed. But, this is not completely effective given how products/services are still being wrongly sold, increased instances of frauds and security issues. So, in future, this activity can get embedded deeper in Fintech solutions, enrich the selling process and also be a mechanism to build trust.

xv. **Community** – This involves having features which enable organizations to connect with specific group/segment in the context of an individual. This has a far-reaching impact on the brand, trust, sales, risk, marketing, PR, communication, etc. This goes beyond basic Social Media integration (as it happens now), and involves creating systems and solutions allowing people to collaborate, guide, enable and transact with each other. This is, therefore, a very big theme and thereby be a key driver for many features in Fintech solutions in future.

xvi. **P2P** – The Peer to Peer (P2P) theme is also going to be a big driver, and somewhere there is good convergence with Social and Community themes too. We have already seen products in P2P lending and even insurance, and this will pick up in future.

xvii. **Connected** – Given the increasing availability and use of connected devices (Mobile, IoT, Sensors, WIFI, etc.). It is imperative to have capabilities and features in a solution that provides real time connectivity and access amongst clients, employees and even communities. So, connected goes beyond just digital connection and also covers access, availability and responsiveness. So, from Fintech perspective an AI-driven Chatbot can also improve connectivity in a big way.

xviii. **More real time** – Being connected people will want information, services and execution which is instant and real time. This leaves scope for various levels of solutions that can be offered to clients and even priced differently, subject to regulations.

xix. **Portability** – Portability enables users to switch between providers of a financial product/solution. It is like transferring your bank account from one bank to another, but retaining the same account number. This involves a larger industry level initiative, given a higher level of collaboration, policy setting, procedures and standardization involved. Portability can also be mandated by regulators for certain segments. In future, this will become more prevalent, easier and be applicable across many more product segments.

xx. **Interoperability** – Interoperability enables seamless interaction between organizations/countries. Like portability this is largely an industry level, tech and/or regulatory initiative. APIs further accelerate interoperability thereby offering tremendous benefits to end users as they can transact smoothly amongst each other. Another area this will benefit is in business continuity, mergers, acquisition and partnerships.

Note: Both Portability and interoperability are key pillars to accelerate Open APIs based digital financial services.

xxi. **User Interface and User Experience (UI and UX)** – Though in vogue for some time now, the relevance and importance of UI and UX has exponentially increased in Fintech solutions. This is because of multiple interfaces, devices, advent of Chatbots, voice-based interfaces, etc. Also, given that most products are getting standardized, increased differentiation based on UI and UX is becoming key to engaging customers.

Note: Both UI and UX go hand in hand and are therefore used jointly. For ease of understanding, UI is basically the elements of the interface medium, for e.g. the app layout, the buttons, icons, fonts, colors, spacing, etc. in a mobile app, while UX on the other hand involves the experience of the user in exploring the product/service, available on the interface and will mostly involve aspects like the accessibility, navigation, interaction, time taken, etc. So, the UI designers create what the UX designer defines in the use journey/flow.

xxii. **Interfaces** – Future Fintech solutions will have to be designed keeping in mind various devices and interfaces viz. portal, mobile, voice, gesture, sensors, wearables, chatbots, videos, etc. Though solutions nowadays are responsive across devices, many still operate in silos. So, the experience is broken for customers, thereby leaving a good scope for innovation/improvement.

xxiii. **Loyalty and Rewards** – Many Fintech solutions differentiate by offering a point linked, loyalty and rewards program. These are largely based on user activity and usage. But this concept actually goes deeper, if one considers Life time Value (LTV) of a customer, and its relevance will rise further in future. Crucial aspect to note here is the effectiveness of the program. As loyalty can be based on product usage (share of wallet and how many products and services used), referrals, other engagements and involvement with the brand. So, rather than just having a points system, there has to be a planned approach with activities to improve loyalty, and ensure that the customer benefits in form of rewards. In credit cards, it has been noticed that many customers do not utilize benefit of their loyalty points, raising questions on the program itself. So, appropriate alerts and communications must be done with customers to improve its effectiveness. Many new business models and startups specializing in loyalty and rewards have emerged, and so existing firms may partner with and integrate with such firms for this. These specialized loyalty partners will create programs in consultation with the Fintech firm, and this will be implemented across the solution based on how the point scoring logic will work. There will also be a marketplace where these points can be redeemed or utilized or maybe customer will be offered some additional services/product against the points.

xxiv. **Gamification** – Another very important future development concerning digital Fintech apps is Gamification. This basically involves creating a game like environment with stages, accomplishments, rewards which engage customers in interacting with/using the solution. This is the next level of evolution in translating Loyalty and Rewards. For e.g. when customer downloads and onboards with a Neo Banking App he is given 10 points, when he does some level of transaction, he is given say 20 points, and once he reaches 50 points by regular usage or by buying new products, gives referrals, etc.

he unlocks a free offer for a credit card. Similarly, there can be many more involving multiple users. Currently some level of gamification is provided by some apps, but it will become more customized and intertwined with the user's interaction and usage of the solution.

xxv. **Partnerships** – The Fintech space of future will largely be propelled to next level through partnerships and alliances. This is also fueled by emergence of open APIs and an intent to offer a seamless value/experience to customers. There can be multiple levels and types of partnerships and we have discussed this aspect in more detail, across various sections in the book.

xxvi. **Emergence of Platforms** – Solutions which were largely specific to a particular functionality/user type are getting combined as a platform. Ecosystems are expanding and involve much more than just employees and customers, and so are the functionalities. Similarly, scope of engagement for external parties like vendors, partners, govt. agencies, service providers, related players is also expanding, and they can be brought to the platform. This is possible with APIs. Hence, platforms are important as they help bring in all involved in the value chain and roll out a comprehensive solution for the customer.

xxvii. **Marketplaces** – Marketplaces are kind of frontend business extension of platforms. They bring multiple buyers and multiple sellers on a same platform. In fact, they are a business model in themselves. For Fintechs, these can be both on business side and technology side (FAM) depending on solution they offer. For e.g., a bank may create a marketplace for car buyers or it may be a lender on some other car platform. Similarly, on technology side, it can create, or be a part of APIs marketplace where its loan APIs are made available (FAM).

xxviii. **Convergence and Bundling of Products across segments** – Another key trend is that financial products are getting integrated and bundled and no longer looked at in isolation, or just for cross sell/upsell purposes. This trend has greatly influenced new business models. For e.g., payments solutions getting linked with lending, bill payments, etc. Similarly, loans and insurance have a lot of synergies.

xxix. **Digital Only offerings** – Fintech solutions are unique in a manner that they can be created, delivered and consumed entirely digitally. This unique characteristic, along with support from ecosystem and technology has spawned a new generation of players like Wallets, Neo Banks, etc., with digital only offerings.

xxx. **Phygital Offerings** – While we have discussed the move towards fully digital Fintech Products and Solutions, there is still good need for Digitally assisted financial products and solutions through physical channels (Phygital). This is driven by customer needs/preferences and sometimes even by regulations. Phygital offerings can thereby be used as a differentiation and offered as premium with a personal touch. So, it is like Investment Advisor/Private Banker who is assisted by Robo Advisory driven investment algorithms, video based consulting etc. Another aspect to consider is Risk of fully digital offerings, and the trust and comfort of Physical Infrastructure and presence. So, phygital is here to stay, albeit in limited form, where digital is used to augment capability of physical resources.

xxxi. **Customized solutions** – Another great ability of Fintechs is that, by leveraging technology, data and analytics, they can offer customized solutions to their customers. This can be tailored to customers' preferences based on products, its features, service requirements, usage and pricing.

xxxii. **Microsolutions and Sachetization** – An interesting theme which expands the sell ability of financial products to existing customers, and widely expands the reach to new segments, is the ability to offer smaller units of the products. Earlier there were reach and cost limitations, but increasingly driven by technology, interoperability and partnerships, the threshold is reducing. For e.g., one can buy travel insurance only for a specific journey, buy smaller units of investments products, remittances for a smaller amount at less cost, etc. Also, for expanding reach of financial solutions in developing world (financial inclusion) this will be a key driver.

xxxiii. **Seamlessness** – One key driver of any Fintech solution going forward will be the seamlessness it offers, i.e. getting over breaks in a process/fulfillment, by integrating/automating the same. Over time this has increased, but there is still scope and thereby Seamlessness will remain key to provide that unbroken experience to customers.

xxxiv. **Omnichannel** – Omnichannel experience for customers was always a utopian thought especially in Financial Solutions. Though this has been addressed to some extent across products, the experience is still broken across services. Despite all this, financial firms are more multi-channel, as many of these are silos. A true Omni channel capability is the one which enables customers to access the product or service across various channels. This coupled with Seamlessness and New interfaces opens up many possibilities for Fintechs and Financial firms to work on.

xxxv. **Beyond Borders** – When European Union decided to have a single payment and settlement regime (SEPA), it opened up a new area for development in payment solutions across Europe. So, this will widen as world gets more integrated and offers good opportunity around payments/remittances, Investments, Insurance etc. While credit cards companies offer some of these capabilities, they are costly and complex. So, the challenge is to create more efficient and cost-effective solutions which are easily accessible. We have seen some Fintechs making cross border forex conversions efficient and cheaper too. So, expect to see a lot more action in areas with Fintech Products and solutions going beyond borders.

xxxvi. **Multilingual** – This will go beyond simple multilingual menus and content to help customers navigate and use a particular financial product or service. With new interfaces like Voice, Chatbots, etc., this will also involve using technologies like NLP and NLU to bring in multilingual experience to customers. Multilingual will be important to expand reach, personalization and engagement with customers for all forms of digital solutions including Fintech. For e.g., remittance solution with customized multilingual capabilities based on user's language. This also implies that linguistic and community skills will be highly sought after.

xxxvii. **Chatbots** – Chatbots are rapidly evolving and playing a big role in engaging customers across Customer Acquisitions and Servicing. The prevalence is more across text-based chatbots but going forward, there will be voice-based bots too. Their complexity and ease of use will rise, with improvement in NLU, NLP technologies, availability of information, multilingual, application of technologies like AI and ML. We also need to keep in mind, that the interaction is more conversational and not transactional (robot like).

xxxviii. **Differential Pricing** – Given the flexibility in packaging and creating a solution that Fintechs offer, the same can be also be priced differentially based on customer segments and needs. In fact, this can be dynamic and evolve based on response and usage. We will increasingly see flexibility in pricing across Fintech Platforms in future.

xxxix. **Consent Architecture** – Given multiple choices and preferences available to customers, high levels of automation and integration that a digital solution offers, it becomes important to have a mechanism to track appropriate approvals (consent) from customers, about various choices he has made or approvals he has provided. Hence, a robust and proven consent architecture is must, both for legal reasons, and to ensure less friction in the digital Fintech ecosystem.

xl. **Embedding** – We are gradually noticing that financial services are getting embedded as part of a larger platform. In fact, we see this being the norm in future, as all solutions are driven by interoperability, open APIs, data sharing and regulations. A whole new range of front-end players will emerge, who will embed financial services as part of their platform. These need not be just financial services players, but others like ecommerce/digital players too who will embed Fintech solutions as part of their platform.

xli. **Open Banking** – Another theme where lot of action is happening is open banking. Open banking is largely an aggregation of some of the themes discussed above, including data sharing, Analytics, Advisory, Open APIs, Ease of transfers (Transactions) and portability between financial products and services. This will fuel a new category of Frontend Players who will offer open banking solutions based on Open data/API access. So, open banking can be both Advisory and Transaction based (a distinction that will emerge as we have discussed earlier).

xlii. **Concierge Services** – We will see many Fintech firms offering concierge like assisted services aimed at engaging and servicing clients. Such services go beyond banking or financial services, for e.g., banks may offer ticketing, booking cabs, dincouts etc. This can be enabled through various partnerships and tie-ups, and can be both in digital and physical form. We already see this happening in a big way.

xliii. **Societal Impact** – Many Fintechs will be focussed at creating societal impact, through products and solutions aimed at Financial Inclusion. We have already seen that technology helps lower costs, improve access, and enables Sachetisation; these will be key drivers here. The other drivers that will be leveraged are community and data. One more small way apps can create social difference is by adding features like donations, crowdfunding, etc.

xliv. **Assurance-Based Services** – We feel that another big differentiator will be assurance-based services like Validation, Verification, Facilitation, Warranties, Servicing, etc. In a digital scenario, these will grow as there is both need and value, and these are also good sources of regular revenues. These will be bundled with core offer like we have extended warranties or servicing package with white goods, others like claims management, card protection, etc.

xlv. **Unbundling and Bundling** – With new technology, partnerships and changing ecosystem in Fintech, Financial Service players are getting unbundled into multiple segments and processes. These segments and processes have enabled many Fintechs based on their specialization and capabilities. We have discussed these in bit more detail in later part of the book viz. Fintech Players – Current and Emerging Players.

Other aspects in Privacy and Security will also be key themes, and we discuss them as below:

xlvi. **Privacy** – Privacy is increasingly becoming a core compliance aspect in the Fintech space. Increased collaboration between firms including sharing of data is subject to lot of concerns, misuse and abuse. Many privacy regulations have come into effect to address these concerns (e.g. GDPR), and many countries are in process of formulating similar regulations. So, while it may be required, privacy has increased costs of non-compliance, and one needs to also build or ensure these features are available in the products/solution.

xlvii. **Security** – Like privacy, security is paramount to Fintech firms, as it is all about trust and comfort. There can be various types and levels of security breaches, which can cause direct financial losses to both customers and firms involved. So, be it unauthorized access, denial of service attack, hacking or other sophisticated means, they are all serious issues, real and present causes of concern. Hence, various levels of security features right from app level, device level, access related, data related, server related, API related, etc. are being packaged and offered to customers as part of the solution.

xlviii. **Frauds** – Frauds have traditionally been a big challenge in financial services. With Fintech, their methods have increasingly become more sophisticated, easier and can have a larger impact too. These involve activities like phishing, social engineering, etc. and also result out of security breaches. So, appropriate measure to first make the users aware, and ensuring that they are proactively alerted and prompted become critical features to counter fraud. Analytics and Artificial Intelligence are also helping counter frauds proactively. We are also increasingly noticing frauds which are low value but high volume and thereby impact a large segment. Being low value and high on sophistication, these can go unnoticed by an individual, and thereby detection and action by Fintech Firms and regulators is needed to protect the customer.

xlix. **Disputes** – With Fintech there is increased partnerships, variation and simplification of solution for client. This has resulted in complexity of products at backend, issues with network, bugs in system, data challenges, jurisdiction/regulatory overlaps, operational challenges, user and processing errors, etc. So, any form of disputes is increasingly complex to resolve. In fact, dispute resolution and claims is an industry in itself, and increasingly we see lot of solutions and services evolve here.

Note: We expect that various regulations, tools, assurance/insurance services will evolve to address these (as mentioned earlier) and this will also open new areas for career professionals.

Technology aspects to be mindful of in future – There have been many recent technologies, fuelling innovation in Fintech. We try to simplify some below.

l. **Big Data** – We have seen data explosion in the digital space with multiple solutions, user-generated data, variety of content, user activity, device data and interfaces etc. So, be it volume of data, its size, speed of data (velocity), types of data (variety) and correctness of data (veracity), etc., the scope of data has become large, and hence it is called Big Data. There are technology, tools and frameworks available to handle big data. A well modelled data framework is very crucial for having effective analytics, AI/ML, NLU and NLP. Big data also opens up possibilities to lower risks, improve efficiencies, know the customers better, and engage with them to offer better products and services.

li. **AI and ML** – Artificial Intelligence and Machine Learning is another technology trend with wide applicability in Fintech. The core to AI/ML solutions is the data, training of the solution on the data, neural networks and models to derive inferences/patterns and act upon them. This involves advanced algorithms in data engineering, statistical analytics, pattern recognition, etc. and can be used for understanding/profiling users and their actions, suggesting/advising to clients, show relevant ads/content, fraud management, etc.

lii. **NLP and NLU** – Natural Language Processing and Natural Language Understanding are the key technologies working behind the scene, when users interact with a chatbot (Voice or text). It involves understanding and making sense of what you have typed or spoken. This can be multilingual and also based on various spoken accents. It is an extension of AI/ML technologies and helps in identifying human uniqueness (like tone, words used, speed, etc., while typing/speaking) and intent. This can be used for better servicing and securing clients. We need to ensure that these technologies are applied in a conversational manner rather than being transactional.

Note: It is important that for AI, ML, NLU and NLP to remain effective and relevant, we need to continuously train the system and keep learning. So, the model cannot be static, else it can be tricked or prove ineffective. Also, such solutions raise ethical and legal challenges too in terms of how they are used (biases, wrong intent, etc.) and their impact (if things go wrong).

liii. **Workflow Automation (WFA) Solutions** – WFA solutions make it easy to create workflows across processes, and are gaining a lot of traction in financial services. In a WFA solution, each process will have input forms, user types and respective rights assigned. Then related external APIs can be integrated in the form, along with documents. On top of that, one can also set rules, limits, formulae, etc. across various parameters in the form, thereby defining the workflow. The ease of use, configurability and faster go to market have enabled wider adoption of such tools.

Another small derivative of such tool is RPA, which is defined as below.

liv. **RPA** – Robotic Process Automation is a smart, easy to use tool that helps in quickly automating human interaction with computer. Manual tasks, activities, and processes which are repetitive in nature and involve actions like Copy, Paste, click on activity buttons and tabs, scroll, delete, alternating between solutions, some computations, etc. can be Automated using RPA. If one has used Macros in excel, this is just a logical extension of similar capabilities, just that it goes beyond one particular app and can automate between various apps, web pages, images (OCR driven), etc. This tool/technology has been increasingly used across processes like account opening, invoice processing, trade processing, customer service, etc. to automate various repetitive tasks. Some Fintech firms have bundled innovative RPA-based bots as part of their solutions too. As these tools become easier to use and are widely prevalent, we expect many small capabilities will keep getting developed and addressed through them.

lv. **Internet of Things (IoT)** – Internet is expanding beyond mobiles and desktops and into many devices which are getting hooked onto the web. These devices in Fintech context could be your self-servicing remote/autonomous kiosks, ATMs, drones, smartwatches and other devices/hardware with specific sensors to capture relevant data/parameters. Mechanical devices are usually managed through actuators and then there are other sensors like image sensors, gyroscopes, accelerometers, altitude sensors, weight sensors, temperature sensors, etc. IoT has therefore opened many used cases for innovation and automation of solutions and services in Fintech. Also, with 5G, IoT driven solutions will witness exponential growth in coming few years.

lvi. **Biometrics** – We have already seen use of Biometric features like Fingerprint, IRIS and Voice. We even have face recognition technology now and all this can be used for User Authentication, Identity, Fraud Prevention, etc.

lvii. **Blockchain** – Blockchain is a technology which stores data securely in blocks. Once a block is full (like a page in a book) then another block gets added, then another to create a chain. It works more like a network where participants can add to the blocks based on their authorization and activity. There are also variations in use cases depending on how open or closed the network/group is. The algorithm and how data is processed and stored in Blockchain adds to security, and supposedly reduces complexity in processing transactions, involving multiple parties and stages. This enhanced level of data security is supposed to lend more trust to a system, which is core to financial services and Fintechs. That is the story as far as using Blockchain as a database. There is another aspect, where Blockchains technology is used for issuing digital currencies or crypto currencies.

This is another area where many use cases have emerged in Fintech. But, it has also been noticed that regulators are usually a bit over cautious and sometimes restrictive about assessing/approving Blockchain use cases/solutions involving Cryptocurrencies.

lviii. **Application Programming Interface (API)** – APIs enable one solution or software or program to talk to another (Send and receive information). They are very important development towards a more connected/integrated Fintech ecosystem. A new era of Open APIs is emerging and enabling innovations and growth of the Fintech ecosystem. We have discussed more on this under FAM.

lix. **Cloud** – With a wider reach of internet, use of browsers, improved bandwidth and data storage capabilities, we have seen emergence of centralized application hosting platforms and infrastructure called Cloud. So, there is no need for client-based installations. These clouds can be Public Clouds (More for open applications), Private Clouds (for dedicated secure users, applications and firms) or Hybrid (Mix of both). Besides, ability to create a platform and single instance of application for all, these clouds also offer other benefits of scalability, security, DR, access to software/hardware options, etc., all at a lower cost and better efficiency. This has resulted in increased adoption of clouds in Fintech too, as this has positive impact on safety, time to market, scalability, ease of development, integrations, costs and ease of management. Clouds largely offer solutions under 3 categories, viz., Software as a Service (SaaS), Platform as a Service (PaaS) and Infrastructure as a Service (IaaS).

lx. **5G** – A strong bandwidth enabled by 5G technology will ensure that better solutions and richer experiences can be delivered to customers and this will also take Fintech to a next level. Many aspects discussed in themes above can therefore be effectively realized with 5G.

lxi. **Web 3.0** – We owe a lot of success in the digital revolution to the Internet, and the way it has shaped the world today. From being mere static links and text on pages (Web 1.0), internet has evolved into a more social and interactive framework (Web 2.0) containing dynamic content, personalization, social media, content beyond text (Graphics, Video and Voice), sharing of content, etc. But in last few years, even this is becoming inadequate, as the scope of Internet increases and more applications, devices, users and resultant data gets added to the net. Enabling technology and devices have also undergone big change with 5G, connected devices (IoT), smart phones/devices, wider usage of cloud, etc. becoming more prominent. Besides, this Web 2.0 also had limitations and concerns around security, fake content, unwanted ads, etc. That is exactly what Web 3.0 is addressing. Web 3.0 has Semantic capabilities (i.e. context is more important than text), supports use of AI, central identity, effective usability and connectivity across various devices, better graphics and other measures to make it safer. However, the most important aspect of Web 3.0 is that it fosters decentralized approach/framework, and this is suitable to technologies like Blockchain and Cryptocurrencies. This implies that with Web 3.0, we will probably see a much deeper integration of financial products/solutions and models driven by community and P2P can be better supported. So, one needs to keep tabs of developments in the Internet space as that can be a key to foster new wave of innovative products/solutions.

lxii. **Augmented Reality and Virtual Reality** – AR and VR as they are known will also be a key technology in Fintech as they can be used in areas like training, user acquisition, advisory, relationship management, etc. So, why not visit a virtual bank and transact? It is very much in realm of possibility.

lxiii. **Quantum** – Quantum computing as the term suggests is a quantum leap from current generation of computing technology. It involves exponential/higher rate of processing. In short, devices and resultant solutions will become smarter and faster with Quantum. Given the relatively initial stages of this technology and its high cost, infrastructure challenges and complexity involved, we have few years before some practical/scalable use cases start appearing. This technology also has wider security implications and hence we need to be observant of what happens here.

Many of the themes and trends as discussed till now are spawning new Fintech firms. Similarly, these themes can also be applied to improve/enhance existing Fintech Product or solutions too. Some of these themes can be applied individually, and give rise to a business case or some need to be applied in combination.

> So, given the Fintech themes discussed we encourage readers to do the following:
> - Take one theme or trend, and identify innovative/new-age Fintech solutions based on them.
> - We can also take any existing Fintech solution and then identify the key themes or trends that are applicable to it.
> - We also encourage users to identify, any new theme or trend and share the same at futurefintechframework@gmail.com

Finally, understanding these themes was necessary, as they enable us in ideation and innovation. So, while we have got some basic understanding of the themes, the key point is **how we can use our understanding of these themes and place them in a structured framework, that will enable us to conceptualize and create futuristic Digital/Fintech Solutions**.

This brings us to Section 2, where we discuss about various components in **3F – Future Fintech Framework**. So, let us understand 3F.

SECTION 02

3F – Future Fintech Framework

3F – FUTURE FINTECH FRAMEWORK

3F is a Futuristic Framework that, when applied, enables us to ideate and create innovative Fintech solutions. 3F can also be applied to improve existing solutions making them future ready. Given that Fintech solutions are getting embedded with other digital economy players like Ecommerce, Online Education, Online Travel, etc. many aspects in 3F can be also be applied to these segments too. We have explained the future enablement of Fintech through 3 key components. These **3 key components of 3F** are:

A. **Fintech Digital Life Cycle (FDLC)** – Any Fintech product or solution will have some key stages in customers' digital journey. This will typically begin with Acquisition of customers, and end with Offboarding. FDLC identifies seven distinct stages and explains possibilities to innovate and improvise at each stage. These seven stages will then serve as a base for storyboarding, UI/UX, features, pricing, defining activities and process flows, for a particular Fintech product or solution.

B. **Fintech Logical Architecture (FLARE)** – Under FLARE, applications have been divided into logical layers, based on their respective functionalities/capabilities. This provides us with a Logical Architecture for creating a Fintech solution.

C. **Fintech API Marketplace (FAM)** – FAM as the name suggests, is a Marketplace for Fintech and related APIs. A place where the API users can come to purchase and integrate various APIs or Solutions from API Providers.

It is our vision that each component of 3F will evolve further to accommodate variety of players, solutions and use cases that may arise in future.

–A–

FINTECH DIGITAL LIFECYCLE (FDLC)

A typical life cycle for a Digital Fintech solution begins with Acquisition of Clients, and goes on till the closure of his account (Offboarding). Under FDLC, we have therefore identified **Seven Key stages in user's progression across the life cycle**. These **Seven stages can be used to** understand various aspects involved to **create wonderful experience and journey for the user**, as they use the solution. This will ensure a profitable relationship with customers in terms of higher share of wallet, Net Promoter Score (NPS) and Life Time Value (LTV). These **FDLC stages are product and solution agnostic,** i.e., they can be applied to most Fintech Products and Solutions. Similarly, **FDLC is also technology agnostic**. So, let us look at the stages in FDLC in pages ahead.

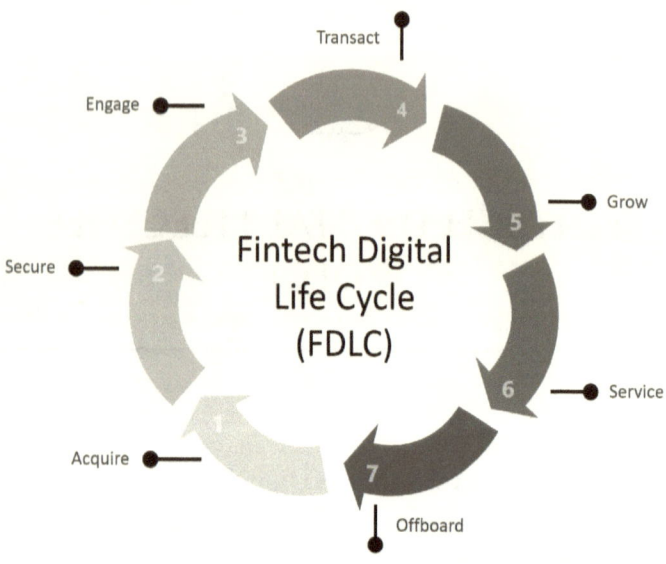

As mentioned, FDLC has seven key stages, which are key to a fulfilling digital journey for a user. This implies that most user journeys will begin with client acquisition, then we need to make them feel secure, engage with them, make them transact, ensure the transaction and relationship grows, we also need to provide them service and finally, there can be situations, where we need to Offboard them. Each of these seven stages have sub stages and we have provided insights and trends, on how we can look to improvise and innovate under each. **The more the movement across the stages is made frictionless and more value is added at each stage the better is the experience.** This is bound to lead to effective customer acquisition, better engagement and retention. It is also important to note that these stages and activities can be fully digital or maybe automated in parts. But at least one user, which is the end user or customer, will always in some way interact with the solution.

Note: We have used the terms User, Prospect, Customer and Clients at various places and they all are related. User is a much broader term and can also include internal users, prospect and client. Prospect is a person who becomes a client after onboarding. Words *Customer* and *Client* mean same i.e. the end customer.

1. Acquire

The Acquire stage is all about channelling clients through Promotions, Leads and Onboarding. So, let us discuss what all we can do under each stage:

a. **Promotions** – This covers whole range of activities to promote a product/solution in both online and offline space. So, be it banner ads, mail campaigns, social media campaigns, mobile ads, videos, chatbots, QR codes for ads/events, feet on street (Mobile and Tab based), prospects calling at call centre, registering on website or other lead generation mechanisms, all are covered. There are tools which enable these activities, and they generate outputs in terms of leads. These tools can also be customized to suit the organization's needs. In Fintech, there may be some user awareness and education required at this stage, and some of it may be mandated by regulations. Also, as part of website, Kiosks, Mobile app one can create various tools and calculators (or gamify them) for comparing products, validating them etc. for e.g. we can have a game for investors to learn on how much will they need to save if they wish to achieve a target. While many such tools exist, the crucial thing is to weave it as part of a funnel culminating into a lead, through various channels or a combination of them.

Note: Before Promotions, we have a whole range of activities under Digital/online Marketing. So, we are not attempting to cover Digital/online Marketing here, our aim is to chart the flow of user/prospect through these marketing efforts into the solution, and specifically highlight aspects about Fintech during promotions.

b. **Leads** – Once leads are generated, they need to be routed effectively to the right channel/dept., location and person. As we generate volumes of leads, and everyone is busy chasing the lead, the efficiency of how a lead is handled, maintained or dropped is quite chaotic. So, there are many solutions with capabilities for lead capture, Validation, dedupe, storage, source tracing, geo tagging, matching, allocation, maintaining history, ageing of leads, classifying nature of their enquiries/needs, follow ups and reports related to the same, etc. These solutions ensure that unnecessary, untimely and mismatched leads are either filtered or handled in a better manner, resulting in better conversion and reduced false positives for Sales. These capabilities can also be incorporated or available as part of new age CRM's/lead management solutions. This is also valid for the Digital funnel, where we may not know source of lead, coupon codes may be truncated, and links may be broken or inappropriately routed. We say this, as there are often gaps in the level of automation between the Promotions stage and lead management. So, the whole experience and stages in the user journey needs to be mapped to cover all possible originations and handling. So, besides keeping the staff motivated, we can engage and create a good impression on prospects by handling the lead well. We can also involve some feedback mechanism here, like having a drop out survey, checking in with a SMS/mail/call, in case lead has not been fulfilled, etc.

c. **Onboarding of Clients** – This stage is important as it involves the actual conversion of a prospect into a customer. It has been observed that, there can be large number of dropouts during onboarding. Also, onboarding involves cost, efforts, impacts motivation of staff, not to mention client's experience. This is further complicated by the fact that, in Financial services, KYC and related compliance need to be adhered too, else costs of non-compliance is high. So, depending on product, lot of data handling concerning client information, different types of documentation, validations, verifications, etc. need to be performed by various internal and external entities at this stage. This has spurned many new solutions in Fintech, which are centred around onboarding.

Onboarding in Fintech goes much beyond just customers and is also needed across Vendors, Partners, employees, specialized professions like Fund Manager, Broker, etc., depending on nature of Fintech and user type. So, the scope of these solutions is really large. Some of the solutions in onboarding are comprehensive and some are in nature of Document scanning/reading tools (driven by OCR capability), Robotic Process (RPA) tools, credit scoring, client profiling, pulling tax and financial records from govt. agencies, credit bureaus, social media tools, AI/ML driven tools for (Online) Background checks, etc. Physical onboarding can also involve capabilities like scheduling, route planning using geolocation, follow ups/reminders for assigned staff etc. Given need for better compliance, lower costs and providing better experience for staff, customer Onboarding is therefore a sweet spot for Fintechs. Another, trend which is happening concerning Onboarding is having a complete digital onboarding capability. This can be driven by digital validation/authorization like Centralized digital Identity, digital signatures/e-sign, biometrics, Video's, OTP's, Devices, Geolocation, Digital Referrals/Social linkages etc. So, be it Wealth Mngt, Insurance, Deposits, Bank Accounts, Loans etc. all offer good scope of improving the onboarding experience for clients. The core aim is to make the process quicker, reduce errors and as much DIY (Do it Yourself) for clients. This implies more automation and transparency at stages wherever possible. Ideally, the best way to approach this is either to list the problem statement or to evaluate new developments in tech and how they can be incorporated to improvize onboarding.

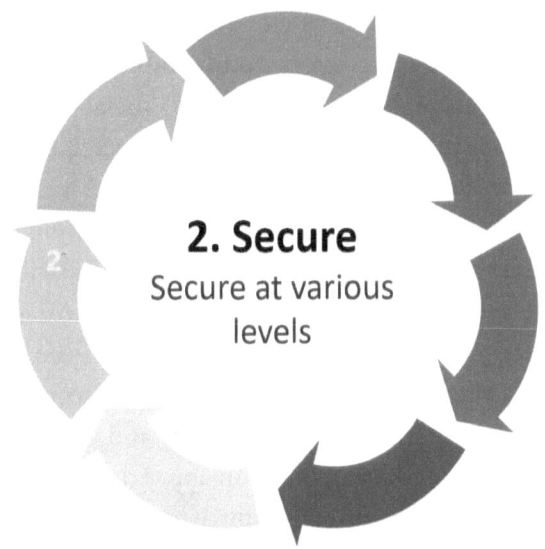

2. Secure

One of the core challenges for a Fintech solution is that, while on one hand it is driven by trust, on the other hand, it is also highly prone to various types of security challenges. These challenges can be at various levels i.e. Data level, Software Level, App level, Functionality Level, Device level, User Level, Others, etc. and have resulted into various security features and functionalities being created. So, features like twin factor authentication, ability to disable cards through app, encryption of data, product level features like transaction limits, cooling/wait periods, alert on activities/transactions, etc. are now available. With use of new technologies like AI and IoT, we can further improvise and keep adding capabilities here like Device Lock, Geo Location, IP Tracking, Embedding Tracking Device, Voice Recognition, face Recognition,

Retina scan, Finger prints etc. These **security measures and features makes users comfortable, builds trust with them** (as highlighted this is very crucial in Fintech), and in many instances, also meet regulatory requirements. There are also technologies which profile users based on how and what they type. Besides compliance to respective laws, having a consent-based architecture may be needed for such security features. There are also insurance and assurance services, etc. which can also be used to give more comfort to the user and secure them. We should also ensure that some audit and verification is done on the user's device when an app is downloaded and installed. This will provide him with comfort. Instead what happens now is, many access permissions are asked without giving reasons, and that is discomforting and thus many times permissions are denied. In fact, different security features can be packaged and priced too, with basic package being free.

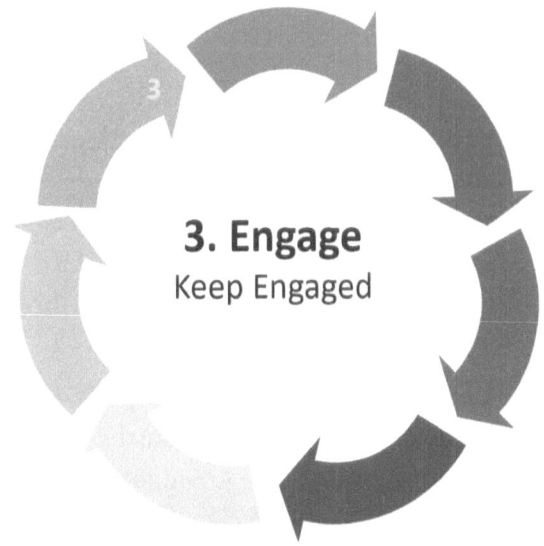

3. Engage

The most important aspect in context of relationship with customers is how you keep engaging with them, so that they keep interacting with the solution regularly. So, if one wants a deeper relationship, a wider and all-encompassing scope of engagement (going beyond just acquiring client and making them transact) is crucial. So, we hereby list a range of activities that can be done within a Fintech solution to keep the customer engaged.

   a. **Profiling** – It is important to profile the client to engage better with him. Nowadays, the interfaces, devices in digital medium and social media offers a range of capabilities that help you profile the client better. Right from what client reads, videos he sees, his actions/

activities, timing, etc. are all available, and these can be used to show him what he likes, make better offers etc. Other traditional ways like questionnaires can be suitably adopted, placed and timed appropriately, using the digital medium. This profiling can also be product specific like there is a risk profiling done for wealth management etc. However, this has to keep privacy aspects in mind.

b. **Communication (Incl. Alerts and Notifications)** – Contextual and timely communication is very important. This can be through various channels like SMS, On App Notifications, mail, call etc. Different types of Alerts and Notifications are highly prevalent today. However, we need to ensure that these are intelligently used, so as not to annoy. Anniversary wishes need to be smartly distinguished from transaction or security alerts. Some control needs to be given to customers about nature of content, frequency and if possible, mode of such alerts. So, it is important to create a map of such alerts and notifications and see if there is an overload, whether some can be grouped, etc. This can consist of Nature of Alert, the Stage, Frequency, Mode, Client Defined, Mandatory or Not, etc. One also needs to keep various interfaces and devices in mind to map these alerts and visualize how they will appear in each.

c. **Tools and Calculators** – We have often seen lot of tools and calculators, as part of various Fintech solutions. These can be a simple loan interest calculating tool, premium calculator, stock filters, charting tools, watchlists, product comparison tools etc. Their purpose could be aimed at keeping prospects and customers engaged or to serve some useful purpose within the context of the solution. However, many of these tools and calculators are standalone, and not effectively presented, to keep customers engaged and use them often. Hence, it is important to weave the tools and calculators effectively to engage with the clients. So, a clear embedding approach is important for each tool and calculator. We can also have some form of conversational approach, gamification that prompts customers to use the tool. So, depending on the journey of respective users, their purpose, use and features need to be well articulated. Tools and calculators can also be used for educating users and improving awareness.

d. **Complementing Solutions** – Another important element to keep customer anchored to a Fintech solution, is to have Complementing solutions/capabilities. For e.g., Tax return Filing, account aggregation capabilities, bill payment etc. This keeps customer engaged to the solution, and ensures he does not go seeking these services elsewhere. So, it is important to create a well-knit complementing ecosystem around your core Fintech product or solution. These are mostly the outcome of partnerships and tie ups, based on API integration.

e. **Community** – Another important anchor for engagement is to have a clear community-based strategy in a Fintech solution. This can be in terms of reaching out to the user's community, to create a community of users and engage your customers to be a part of the same. This serves many purposes and goes beyond just engagement, relationship and affinity and into areas like influence, referrals, new sales, events, preferences, trends, public relations etc. One can also link use of Social Media, P2P features as part of community-based strategy. So, like having a trader's discussion forum in a trading app, tax planning forums in a wealth app, Features like follow, some P2P capabilities etc.

f. **Content** – We consume a variety of content while using any solution. These can be in form of simple inputs explaining the solutions, including aspects like FAQ's, or in some places content itself can be a product, say like a research report. Nowadays it is no more just about written content. So, use of graphics, interactivity, video, audio etc. needs to be considered. Also, in this era of social media, compliance, privacy etc. one needs to be careful about handling of content, including complexity of user generated and multilingual content. So, what we wish to emphasize is, the use of content as part of a broad strategy involving News Letters, community, subscription/tie ups with journals, use of blogs, Video/you tube channel, tutorials, education etc. So, both at content level and technology level like RSS feeds, compression, formats and formatting, presentation, etc. we need to have a clearly articulated approach/policy to deal with content. Finally, given the breadth and depth of content available today, it is very important to be able to classify, tag and search content, as it is applicable and key to many stages.

g. **Events** – The digital medium offers us a good mechanism to organize events both online and offline. So, ranging from promotions, community building, awareness/education or simply entertainment, we can now conceptualize and roll out events quickly using digital tools. Also, events as a strategy, goes a long way in strengthening the bond and deepening the relationship with prospects and customers. It can also be a good tool to increase the size of and affinity within community. We already see free ticket for shows, investor education events etc. being organized. Today, one needs to have these event capabilities embedded as part of an app. So, be it creating an event, holding webinars, enrolling people, sending reminders to attend, feedback or polls during event etc. many things can be done.

h. **Marketplace** – Financial organizations leveraging Fintech should also keep a Marketplace based approach, as that will be a key driver of growth. The biggest advantage of a marketplace is that it provides an entire ecosystem under one place. There can also be end to end digital fulfilment, based on how deeply the marketplace is integrated. So, marketplaces can be for a product or around it, say a marketplace with listing of homes with fulfilment of home loans. One can also look at marketplace as a P2P capability, like renting a home. Similar marketplaces can be for car, consumer durables, etc. Firms can create these marketplaces themselves or they can tie up with an existing marketplace. Also, partnerships and alliances will be key drivers of marketplace, of course led by an API driven open architecture/ecosystem and technology.

i. **Search** – Search is not just a feature. It is actually a crucial activity which the user performs at various stages while using a solution. A true search feature should therefore be very intuitively embedded in the user journey. Today, search goes beyond just text, it can be voice, audio or image based searches too. Another area one neglects are the search results, where emphasis must be on contextual results (use AI), and again it should lead to some conclusive action by customer. Some form of feedback (either obtained or automatic) needs to be there, to increase the effectiveness of search. Going forward, a new hybrid form of search will emerge, based on Big Data, Conversational AI, ML, Voice Recognition etc. Also, search, its results and advisory go hand in hand, though one needs to be careful about how the journey is constructed, keeping compliance in mind (especially in Fintech). Search also helps profile the customer and learn about his habits, behaviour and preferences. So, one needs to always keep in mind what the customer is looking for and whether he got it. This iterative loop with improved effectiveness, convenience and relevance of search results will define success of a search feature.

j. **UI and UX** – We have already briefly touched upon the relevance of UI and UX. Here we talk about different aspects UI and UX to keep users engaged. One crucial aspect will be personalization in terms of content, look n feel, etc. This will include capabilities like dashboarding, calendar views, bucketing of activities, social and activity view, etc. UI and UX can also be changed based on some event like birthday, festival etc. Another area of emphasis will be developing suitable UI and UX for Voice-based solutions as, given the convenience, that is how future interactions are more likely to happen. In fact, some principles about contextual call to action needs to be there. The navigation has to be simple and intuitive. Predictive capabilities using AI can be built, to generate most likely range of actions by customers and make suggestions. The UI and UX thereby becomes more personalized and dynamic. Ability to drive attention, translate into action, limited time to search, navigate, engage, interact and balancing all that with various features, will therefore be key. So, incorporating Design Thinking principles and frequently iterating the design and customer journeys and updating UI and UX will also be needed.

k. **Gamification** – As explained earlier, gamification is another key element in engaging customers to frequently use the solution. So, we need to bring in elements of Games by building stages around usage and consumption of various product and features in the solution. Every action at each stage, will involve some point being rewarded to the user. On achieving certain points and/or crossing some stage or level the customer is rewarded. Reward can be in different forms for e.g. some service/product is made free, or the points redeemed, limits enhanced. Features unlocked etc. Also, gamifications can begin from the time the customer onboards for e.g. he can be asked to provide some references or share with friends and earn some points or get some value-added service free. In fact, onboarding and free product usage can be an outcome of a game (Promotion) itself. For e.g. We already see many apps stating that onboarding/account opening will give you some points.

l. **Analytics** – Analytics present a more actionable insight concerning data and provide a sense of control and transparency too. Hence, they add greatly to engagement aspect of a solution. Also, when we talk of analytics it involves the graphical representation of data in terms of charts and graphs as Images are more impactful. So, something like top performing portfolios, high impact stocks, etc. can be engaging analytics. Others like you have completed your account opening in 48 hrs and are thereby rewarded 30 points. This is gamification based on analytics and is also engaging.

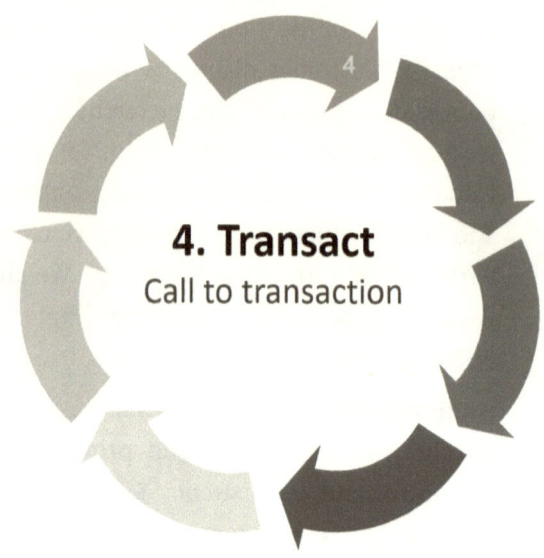

4. Transact

The main objective of any Fintech platform is that the customer eventually uses the platform to transact i.e. mainly use (buy or even sell) the core products/services. Thus, as the customer onboards, feels secure and is effectively engaged, he then has to transact and that too reasonably often. Else in the Fintech space, an account with no transaction turns up being cost. Transactions are thereby directly linked to actions which generate revenue, and thus becomes more important. These economics may not apply to Startups which are on client acquisition spree initially (so free offers etc.), but eventually the economics will catch up. Hence, it is prudent to not lose sight of this objective. With this in mind, let us discuss certain key measures we can take, to ensure that the client effectively transacts on a Fintech platform.

a. **Packages** – Smartly packaged solutions suited to the customer, ensure a high level of conversions/transactions. The advantage is that, since the package suits the needs of the customer, he will decide quickly and pay for the package. For example, prepackaged payments plans, viz. Plan A (Suited for high transactions number), Plan B (Suited for High value transaction), Plan C (Suited for average size transaction). Similarly, we can have Bank accounts created as packages like Executive (for business men), Golden Glow (Senior Citizen), Aspire (Students). These bank accounts can have various features specific to the category. It is not that this is not being done now, just that with technology it is easier to create and manage these packages, and we can create many variations, add more features and benefits. Also, besides preconfigured packages, customers should be able to choose features and create his own package/solution (Customized Packages). This Do It Yourself (DIY) capability gives customers lot of empowerment, alternatively if he is assisted he feels privileged. Even, his dedicated relationship manager can do it for him. We can add gamification to packages for e.g. upgrade to a better package. Packages go hand in hand with features, related benefits and Pricing too. Also, in certain segments, there may be guidelines or regulations concerning creation of packages.

b. **Bundling with other products/solution/offer** – Another intelligent way to encourage customers to transact is to bundle products and solutions of relevance. This goes slightly beyond creating packages and involves complementing solutions being offered as part of an extended option to core package. Even discount coupons as a result of some arrangement/tie ups can be part of this.

c. **Pricing and Discounting** – It is important to get the pricing right for customer to act, else they can get into comparison mode (for some type of products) and not transact. Only by packaging and bundling solutions at right price, will help create a win-win offer. There can be discounts based on Life Time Value of clients (Usually depends on a long relationship/loyalty), renewal discount, theme/occasion-based discounts/offers that help in driving transactions. The digital world is full of free trials, discounts etc., but these must largely be used during client acquisitions or incentivizing dormant customers to transact more. We need to ensure a good balance between value delivered and cost, besides being aware of what competition is doing. Any approach which is not sustainable in long run, inconsistent and not in financial capability should be avoided while pricing/offering discounts. One robust mechanism is to levy a flat annual charge, which at least covers the cost of the solution/platform, or guarantees some minimum level of income per user. Though all this and many more methods can be part of a broader marketing/pricing strategy, which is beyond our scope.

d. **Timing the Offer** – Needless to say, it is important to get the timing of any offer right, as that improves the chances of customers accepting the offer, and transacting. Technology helps in a big way here, i.e. based on analysis of trends, user behaviour (based on profile and past data), social media, geolocation analysis, related situations and events, we can better time the offer and remind to customers. For example, many banks and card companies offer discount on restaurant bills and even print large booklets for the same. But can customers remember all the relevant offers, and that too for so many restaurants? So, ideally there can be a feature, where customer is prompted as he visits a particular restaurant (where offer is valid), based on geolocation tag of the restaurant. Another way to do this is, if Customer is planning for dinner outside and enquires on the search bar, he is accordingly suggested restaurants based on best suited offers. So, why not have such features in the Fintech apps. This will increase transactions. Such capabilities can be rendered with good UI and UX (including alerts, popups etc.) and help to present and place the offers appropriately for effective call to action. Such efforts/features are however subject to appropriate privacy, disclosure and consent about accessing and analyzing data for the purpose.

e. **Contextual Call to Action** – As we have highlighted earlier, one need to ensure that call to action (ability to Buy/Sell) is smartly embedded across all enabling features in the solution (Viz. Content, Analytics, Tools and Calculators etc.). In fact, the UI/UX and related journeys must be conceived in such way that there is contextual call to action or shall we say call to transaction.

f. **Pre-Approved Offers** – Pre-approved implies that there is benefit to customer in terms of Value and Faster process. They are a very nice way to Cross Sell and Upsell to existing customer. Such offers make the customer feels both privileged and also perceives less hassles to accept and proceed with the offer. So, one needs to ensure customer has to enter minimal info, and the steps are also less while designing a pre-approved offer.

g. **Checkout Experience** – Every transaction has 2 phases; one is the actual transaction and the other is the payment. This last stage of payment is thereby core to the whole buying experience. We need to ensure that this process is smooth, and without procedural, technical or user journey related complications. So, a well embedded and solid payment and lending capability during checkout is crucial. It must enable multiple options for customers to Borrow and/or Pay. Also, remember payment can both be made/or received in case of certain financial products. Many new Fintech solutions like Buy Now Pay Later have emerged here, and usually such Fintech solutions are embedded as part of a transaction platform.

h. **Incentive** – One crucial transaction enabler is incentive to staff, as they drive positioning and sales to customers/prospects in many channels. So, from a design perspective, aspect like Staff codes (For incentive) and journey involved as above may be relevant to be captured. Incentives can also be offered to distributors, agents and even extended to clients too. So, appropriate hierarchy and incentive sharing must be built in.

i. **Gamification** – The gamification theme stays relevant during transaction stage too. We can gamify in a manner, such that the customers transact more. We can see somewhat similar happen with credit card points. So, the more you spend, more points you gain. Similarly, in an online trading system, we can have a leader board of most successful traders and other traders can follow the leaders. Such capabilities can be anonymized to take care of privacy whilst rewarding the actual user. Similarly, gamifying all bill payments through a banking app can be one objective. You can also gamify the incentives for employees.

5. Grow

A typical client funnel involves Acquisition of Clients, securing them, engaging them and ensure client transacts, but that is not the end. Success lies in further steps, which ensure that your relationship with client widens and deepens, and they are rewarded for the same. This is exactly what the Grow stage is all about, as Reward and Grow go hand in hand. Let us discuss some important aspects under this stage as below:

    a.   **Cross Sell and Upsell** – This involves Cross selling and Up selling solutions to customers, where they already have a relationship. In cross sell, we usually sell another product/solution, but upsell is more like offering clients a better alternative product/package. But to be effective, we need to base such cross sell and upsell offer on some need or rationale, and also time them well. This is where technology helps to ensure higher wallet share.

b. **Upgrade** – Another good way to make the client feel special is by upgrading him to a premium service/package. This can be based on some criteria, like how old is the relationship, what products he uses, his activity, transactions and financial aspects like income generated etc. Upgrade is like a privilege being extended for free (based on criteria), whereas Upsell is largely a paid transition. We should not use upgrade too often; else upgrade will lose its relevance. Upgrade can also be a reward of gamification as discussed earlier. A feeling of having earned it or being rewarded also helps deepen relationship with clients.

c. **Loyalty Programs** – A strong loyalty program helps anchor the relationship with clients on the platform, and has to be so designed. This goes beyond one off discount and offers (as covered in Transact) and designed more as a Lifecycle than a single journey. Core to a loyalty program are the loyalty points, and of course as has been pointed early, we can use gamification in Loyalty Programs.

d. **Curated Rewards** – Loyalty programs must be linked to a well curated reward marketplace. The rewards must be thoughtfully put up to match the customers' needs and preferences.

e. **Referrals** – Referrals are a good way to grow the relationship with the client as well as expanding the client community by leveraging the network effect (more so if client is an influencer). Financial products being trust based, the impact of referrals is much better and strong. So, one needs to ensure proper incentivization to clients for referrals and technical aspects like use of referral codes, journey involved need to be considered. Referrals imply the confidence the client has in your product/solution. Another, good way to improve effectiveness of referrals is identifying influencers.

6. Service

Another crucial pillar useful to keep clients satisfied is the level of Service and Support provided. With newer technologies, Fintech can automate a lot of activities and processes, to improve access, response times, reduce errors and costs. Some key aspects in Service and Support for Fintechs are highlighted a below:

   a. **SaaS based platforms** – There have been emergence of cloud-based platform which provide helpdesk support (phone, mail, chats, etc.), automated ticketing and related features aimed at providing client service and support. These tools provide end to end tracking and status of resolution too.

b. **Chatbots** – Automated Text and Voice chatbots are proving to be force multipliers for answering/resolving client queries. With AI and ML these chatbots can go beyond standard servicing for clients and ensure better engagement, response time and client satisfaction. But, like all other features, the journeys here need to be intelligently conceived and created.

c. **Social Media Tools** – Social Media platforms and tools like WhatsApp can be integrated and leveraged for servicing clients. Many SaaS platforms also provide social media plugins and chatbots as part of their offering.

d. **Client Reporting and Analytics** – Automated client reporting and analytics are enriching the entire client servicing experience. Besides, standard PDF based reports and visual enhancements by using intelligent charts and graphs, there are innovations which provide video-based reporting too.

e. **Surveys and Feedback** – An important tool to gauge the effectiveness of your products, solutions and servicing is through regular Surveys and Feedbacks. Many tools are available and we can integrate these effectively in the service cycle. Here, it is important to convey a benefit to customer from past surveys, and also communicating changes effected post the current survey. This feedback loop is often missing, and hence survey participation is less.

Many a time, Surveys are also not appropriately placed and annoying. So, we need to tackle these issues to have an effective survey and participation.

f. **Education and Awareness** – Another important aspect, especially in a DIY digital environment, is ensuring that the customer is better educated and aware of various aspects of the solution. This will ensure that he needs less servicing or support. Another way to look at this is, if a customer frequently calls for a particular matter and the call centre agent explains everything to him. But will he remember everything? So, it is good to send across a crisp infographic, video or reading material which he can refer to and does not need to call again for the same.

g. **Search** – We already have FAQ's in many portals but then one has to search for the question and make sense of the answer. A well embedded search feature linked with curated content (relevant to Service and support) is also useful.

h. **Remote Access and Screen share type tools** – Such tools help engage with clients especially in context of any difficulties (technical or otherwise) clients face while using the solution. Agents can remotely join client's session and guide them. This facility can also be used by Relationship Managers/Advisors, to conduct client sessions for aspects like investment performance, relationship reviews, etc.

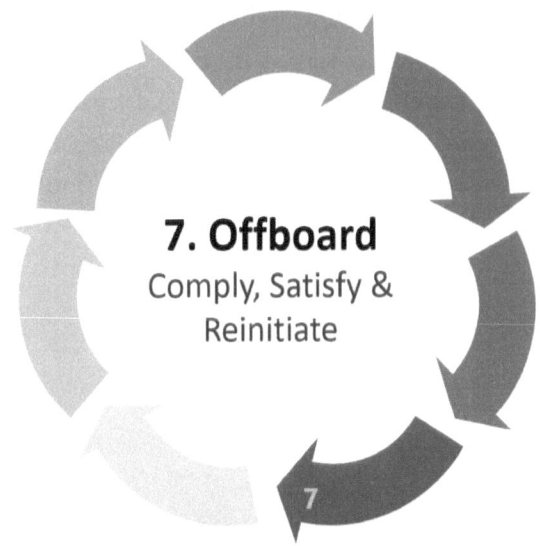

7. Offboard

Offboard is the last leg of a Customer's Journey with a financial firm. This usually involves handling the closure of the customer's account, but also goes beyond. Given privacy, compliance and Fraud management standpoint this is a very crucial step. It is therefore important to understand the reason for offboarding. It could be driven by internal/compliance reasons, or it could be initiated by client because he is unhappy with services, has better alternatives, seldom uses the services, or has finished using the service (say loan is repaid) etc. So, the process for each is different, but underlying is to communicate and make the entire activity as smooth, irrespective of the challenges or reasons to offboard. An opportunity to keep engagement with client, a parting gift/reward, some referrals should also be considered as part of this exit journey. In complex solutions like Loans, the journey may involve collection/recovery as the final leg to closure, and they open entirely different operational/legal challenges. Also, offboard can be a good time to make a pitch for other services and maybe initiate a new relationship.

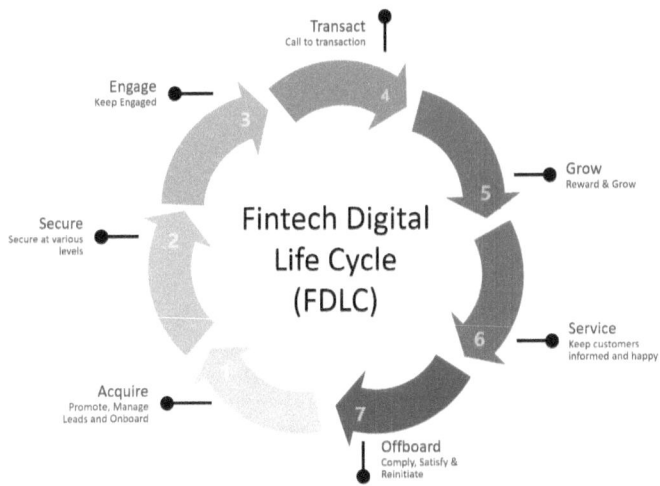

So, as we have seen, irrespective of product or solution, most user journey needs will encompass the above stages, starting from Acquire, Secure, Engage, Transact, Grow, Service and finally Offboard. Within each we have tried to identify the relevant trends and key aspects that need to be considered to make the Fintech solution/platform very effective.

So, given the earlier FDLC stages we encourage readers to do the following:

> - If you are planning a new solution or product in Fintech, then consider running them through FDLC stages. This will ensure that you have a nicely packaged proposition. It will also help in making the whole user experience complete and engaging.
> - If you are further interested in FDLC and wish to share some insights on the same, you can share the same at futurefintechframework@gmail.com

While we have seen various stages of the journey which any product/solution needs to undergo to make the experience very rich and engaging and eventually profitable, another crucial aspect of the 3F framework is the FLARE (Fintech Logical Architecture).

–B–

FINTECH LOGICAL ARCHITECTURE (FLARE)

Fintech Logical Architecture (FLARE) categorizes different system capabilities for a Fintech solution, across various logical layers. FLARE has been aligned with possibilities as discussed in FDLC. FLARE can support as a base for System Development and enable evolution of a Fintech platform in a modular manner. APIs from different layers will talk to each other and the architecture will also consist of database, Workflow engine and frontend/interface for users. To ensure all the APIs function according to plan (as and when needed) an API' orchestration layer will be required. The following are various layers in FLARE:

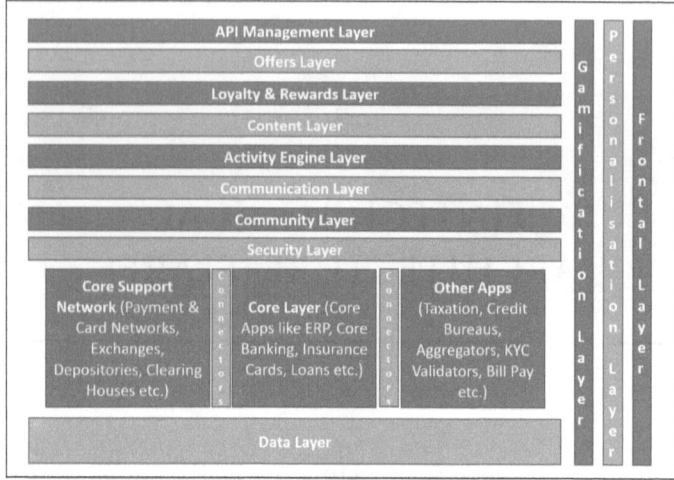

FLARE Diagram

Let us now look at some details for each of the logical layers in FLARE.

1. Core App Layer

The core app layer consists of apps like ERP, Core banking, Product specific core apps etc. say for Cards, Loans, Insurance, Trading App etc. which may exist. Though we think that all this will be replaced by one core application in future. In this Core various product groups will be created based on accounting taxonomies, hierarchies etc., So, a grouping of all accounts will be created for the respective product, pricing, Interest, incentives, discount codes etc. Even user level accounts will be created. These accounts will maintain certain limits from risk and management aspects. They need to be kept in mind while configuring pricing for various products across respective segments of customers. Also, at the core app level, various user roles and each user is created and maintained. Basically, core app will cover accounting, products and users. Core Layer will also have connectors to payment systems, exchanges, card networks, clearing houses etc.

2. Other Applications

Other applications are usually partner apps or supporting apps, whose API will be consumed as part of the offering to the user. For. E.g. the APIs from Credit Bureau for loans, some APIs in KYC process, APIs for Account Aggregation, GOVT apps, Taxation etc. These services may be operationally required, or be a value add to clients.

3. Data Layer

Data layer is very important, as today we have variety of data across different formats available to us or getting generated. Data needs to be cleansed, classified, arranged, stored and analyzed. This data can pertain to Product, Apps, Users (Including Customers), Activity and Transactions. We even have data coming in because of IoT and different devices. There are lot many data tools/solutions that are available, and we will classify them is 4 buckets viz. Data Collection/Assimilation Tools, Data Storage, Data Analytics and Reporting solutions.

> **Data Collection/Assimilation tools** will basically collate data and pass on to data storage. Usually involves data analysts.

> **Data Storage** – This is where data is stored. For a system with various parameters and capabilities, the database needs to be intelligently designed. This must be in line with various data sets available and their correlation with entities, activities involved etc. Basically, involves activity like database design, warehousing of data etc. This activity is very important but is often done in an adhoc manner. This does not make the database efficient and their potential is not maximized. So, due importance must be given to this aspect, and database overhaul or redesign, must be done at regular intervals.

> **Data Privacy and security** – Various aspects related to data privacy need to be factored in a solution. They are largely in nature of Data Storage, encryption, display, masking/anonymizing data, etc.

- **Reporting** – A very basic but important part of data is reporting. This can be in nature of Compliance/Regulatory reports and also client reports. There are various point solutions usually available in this regard and some are inbuilt in the database itself.

- **Data Analytics** – The most visible and talked about aspect of data is the Analytics, and visual representation of the same. There are various tools and solutions available today for the same. These analytics can be simple or they may involve advance statistics or application of AI/ML especially in case of Predictive and Prescriptive Analytics. These tools allow creation of various models based on statistics and rule sets, for analyzing data and graphically representing them. Often, many firms face challenge in implementing an analytics project as they have not done proper data storage or have not designed their databases well. So, while they seek Data Scientist, they actually need smart data engineers to design the data, then analytics becomes very easy.

Note: Data is a very crucial element of every system, so ideally if the readers are not technically trained in databases, then they should familiarize with some basics, viz. different data types (Structured, unstructured, semi structured etc.) data sources, databases, Relationship between entities and data sets, basics on analytics and data related statistics. This basic knowledge helps while creating a solution and interacting with technical data engineers and scientists. Many projects and systems fail or do not perform effectively, as they are not aligned with the data, data is not available or because of incorrect data. Data mapping and linking should happen before integration else while system may work, it will not be correct and we cannot effectively correlate, track and manage.

4. Security Layer

The importance of security in Fintech solutions and related developments has earlier been highlighted in FDLC. Here, we will touch upon same aspects and bring in additional insights from an architecture perspective. In FDLC (Under Secure) we have understood that security happens at various levels right from Data, Hosting, OS Level, Application, Functionality, Device, User actions etc. We also would highlight few specific aspects to be kept in mind as below:

- An AI based engine that will provide security based on complex patterns, and then an enhanced version can be offered at a price too.
- A consent-based architecture can be used to provide alerts in case of sensitive data being accessed.
- Data and analytics related to security thereby needs to be built in.
- Other aspects related to Cybersecurity viz. availability of system, compromise to systems,

injection of malware, trojans etc. need to be taken care of.

- Proper Audit and remedial measures need to be in place in case of security issues.
- It is also important to note that most applications in their own way will also have some form of security built in. In such a case we need to create a framework, to keep a tab on them and use them effectively.
- Another area to be cognizant is that proper penetration testing of an app must be done. All scenarios must be tested (automated testing only helps in basic), need to ensure that all endpoints are secure, ports are not left open, data is encrypted at device level, transmission and storage.

5. Community

The community layer consists of various technical solutions and capabilities enabling social media integration, peer to peer sharing, referral, session sharing etc. which may need to be built or integrated.

6. Communication Layer

This layer technically enables/integrate various communication solutions viz., mail, SMS, chatbots, etc. Even aspects like Alerts, Notifications and Broadcast capabilities are covered. Will also cover the gateway interfaces, scheduling, routing, etc. Even managing whether communication has reached clients and responses routing etc. will be handled here. This is very important again from compliance and servicing perspective and providing a seamless experience to customers.

7. Activity Engine

Activity Engine allows creation of various workflows which are either completely digital/automated, or involve manual processing. The workflow will consist of a form with fields, where values can be input, documents attached and validated. We can also embed various internal and external APIs to create the workflow, define which entities are involved, set rules, logic and computations for progress of workflow, parallel activities involved, etc. The advantage is that it is easier to make changes to workflow (like adding, modifying and deleting the steps, document requirements, process logic and people at various stages) and manage them. Workflows can be created for various activities and processes like account opening, transaction entry, loan processing, etc.

8. Content Layer

Content is becoming a great engagement tool, and is also a driver for contextual call to action, resulting in transactions. It may also be important from compliance perspective. Content layer will basically be a unifying layer to:

> ➢ Gather content from internal, partner or external sources – We have already highlighted aspects like video-based content, besides textual

content, multilingual, different formats, compression etc. in FDLC
- Manage them i.e. store and tag them (with categories/subcategories and key words)
- Make content available to end user, which also includes ability to run and manage preferences, subscriptions, etc.
- Capabilities to handle and share content are also important

9. Loyalty and Rewards Engine

This layer specially handles the complete Loyalty and Rewards capability, which are linked to client relationship, usage of various products, events and transaction volumes etc. The key to loyalty and reward system is that, it should be able to have unit wise count (Point scoring system) across parameters applicable under Loyalty program. Ability to define Loyalty categories and rules. Interfacing with external programs based on APIs need to also be considered.

10. Offers Engine

The offers engine is where offers can be created based on some business logic, and linked with customer types and transactions. This layer will thus contain various parameters which can be selected and defined to create an offer for a specific time duration and customer type. So, while offers can be created on business need/promotion basis (focus on Product and Transaction), Loyalty and rewards is more long term (Focus on Customer).

11. API Management Layer

This layer is needed to manage and orchestrate various APIs and also cover aspects like APIs Availability, Consistency, Readiness and Scalability.

12. Gamification Layer

Just like in workflow, the gamification layer will help define various stages, attributes/parameters, that need to be tracked to score points (defined as an attribute itself) and unlock a particular feature/reward (another parameter) in a game. So, there needs to be an ability to create the flow, calculate points, link with outcome etc. There also needs to be an intelligent way to weave a game as part of an interesting story/engagement, and manifest it with intuitive UI. Besides this there can be P2P/community-based gamification and performance-based gamification too. For e.g. performance of a portfolio of invested stocks, where the best performing portfolios are ranked.

13. Personalization Layer

The personalization layer is very critical as it provides max control of the solution to the customer, he feels empowered and trust improves. So, users can define their preferences, look – n – feel, layout and even privacy, etc.

14. Frontal Layer

The Frontal Layer will cover aspects like Interfaces, devices and related UI and UX. Various features and capabilities of the solutions will be enabled and displayed for appropriate interaction and call to action. This will be done based on user stories/journeys defined.

Note: The above layers have been mentioned based on current understanding and categorization. It is possible that some of these layers can be merged with other layers, and evolve depending on what options/technology is available. Hence, we call it a logical architecture.

> So, given the FLARE layers, we encourage readers to do the following:
>
> ➤ Apply FLARE to create their own logical architecture, for their own Fintech Product or Solution.
>
> ➤ Also, feel free to share your feedback and insights on FLARE by mailing at futurefintechframework@gmail.com

---

FLARE Features – The following are some of the features of FLARE

Modular Architecture

FLARE will facilitate incremental growth, i.e., it allows for both horizontal and vertical enhancements to Product, features, solutions, partners. An API driven platform enables easy integration to both internal and external solutions, i.e., Plug and Play capability.

Highly Secure

Security is built into every element of the platform i.e. at Backend, Frontend, Product Feature, Device level, Authentication, etc. Besides reducing incidences/possibilities of security breach/frauds, this also results in increased trust, better adoption and usage of the solution.

An outside-in platform

FLARE is conceptualized as a Frontend to Backend solution, i.e., the platform is designed based on what you want to offer end users/customers, and then working backwards on various elements that will be needed to enable. It also implies a higher emphasis on aspects like Personalisation, Customization, Profile/Device based user journeys, Omnichannel experience etc. This outside-in approach enables faster go to market.

Engagement and Call to Action

Every aspect of FLARE is aimed at contextual user engagement, and resultant call to action. On one side customer tends to benefit with better features, solutions, pricing, rewards etc. and the Bank tends to have a better share of wallet to the customer, increased ROI and profitability.

Collaboration

FLARE is a highly collaborative platform with emphasis on, social/community features between the Bank, its customer and amongst customers. This results in better usage, referrals, feedback and enables the platform to establish a personal relation/credibility between the users.

High Automation and DIY

FLARE features high level of automation, so interaction between users are digitally augmented/enabled. There is a high level of DIY (Do It Yourself). This results in faster customer fulfilment and a feeling of being in control.

Cross Channel Interactivity

FLARE will also ensure that an activity can be performed across various channels, with cross interactivity. This will be done keeping experience, convenience and safety in mind. An example is use of QR code on ATM (Instead of entering PIN number) through the mobile phone.

– C –

FINTECH API MARKETPLACE (FAM)

The Fintech ecosystem is crowded with different types of players, providing various solutions. We can see Financial Players, Technology Firms and even Non-Financial Players offering a variety of products, solutions and services. Besides, it is not just various products, solutions from different Vendors/Service Providers, there are multiple types of users too.

This makes the whole process of evaluating and selecting various solutions, negotiating with vendors/providers, partnerships, onboarding process amongst each other, integrating them and going live, etc. very time consuming and complex. This is because users have to manage multiple Vendors/Service Providers. So, given that various permutations and combinations are possible, comparing and making choice becomes difficult. Also, it is not just the users, but the Vendors/Service Providers too face difficulties in terms of higher time to market and costs.

In today's times, where firms are adopting more of cloud technology and API-based integration with external solutions and Service providers, we have seen emergence of various API Stores or API Platforms, which primarily list different APIs and their documentations. This trend is starting to pick up in Fintech over last few years. But, most of the existing API Platforms, are usually mere listings with some search capabilities, and requiring some technical understanding and support for consuming and configuring the respective APIs. Also, limited APIs are listed, many not across categories and the whole process of agreement and onboarding of vendors/solution providers is still complex and offline.

Hence, we foresee that some of the above challenges will get addressed, with the emergence of a more mature and open API Marketplace, called Fintech API Marketplace (FAM). FAM will thus enable Single Point Onboarding (of users), ability to compare and select various APIs (Based on products and services they wish to offer), complete Onboarding (Vendors), Ability to configure and integrate APIs easily, create user journeys and go live with end solution in form of a Mobile App, Web Based and Voice-Based Platform. Since, APIs will be available at a centralized Marketplace, their path to standardization will also accelerate.

We foresee that FAM will be ready to deploy for simple use cases. For some complex use cases and business scenarios, there may be some technical work required, but that too will reduce or become negligible as FAM evolves. Hence, one can thereby start a Fintech or embed Financial services into their existing solution rapidly using FAM. This is just similar to how we can now quickly build a website. For e.g., the way we simply book a domain, buy a hosting plan, select the Content Management Framework and template, integrate related features/APIs (For e.g., forms, mails, chats, ecommerce, personal, social media, payments, RSS feeds, etc.), add content, images and our website is ready to be published. We can either do each of these tasks on our own, or take a complete package from some provider. Same way we can create our own Fintech Solutions (Neo Bank, Payment Solution, Robo Advisor, Aggregator, Loan Provider, Card, etc.) or embed Fintech APIs into our solutions via FAM. We have explained with some examples a little ahead in this section.

1. Who Will Create FAM's?

Many existing Players Viz. Large Financial Firms, Financial Exchanges, Core Tech Providers (Like Core Banking, Payment Companies etc.), Web Hosting, cloud Providers, SAAS companies in Financial Services, Big Tech Players, Aggregators, etc. who currently offer some related APIs as part of their closed ecosystem, will gradually morph into a more open FAM. They will upload their APIs, Define API use cases, Documentation, Pricing, modalities and details required from users to purchase and go live, including agreement, etc.

FAM will in a way enable organizations to create their own architecture, as proposed in previous chapter on Fintech Logical Architecture (FLARE). So, basically FAM will enable with component APIs, which can be used to create FLARE (which is like a complete Fintech stack), or to embed specific products or modules into an existing solution.

FAM will benefit these players immensely as:

a. Faster Product and Go to Market cycle.
b. It will greatly reduce Go Live efforts.
c. It will be a big win for early FAM's, who evolve with the FAM ecosystem, as they will get deeply embedded with all partners.
d. FAM's can lead to faster standardization of APIs, which is a challenge now.
e. Expand the market, as FAM will spawn a broader set of providers and users.

f. Make Partnerships quicker and smoother. For e.g., a core solution provider can partner with others like a Loyalty program player, Content Provider, etc.

2. Key FAM Constituents and Features

Providers	Categories of APIs and Solutions	Features on FAM	Users of FAM
Tech Cos	Multi Stacks	Publishing of APIs	Individuals/ Professionals
BFSI Firms	Core Solution APIs	Single Point onboarding of all participants	Communities, Groups/ Associations
Exchanges	Product Focussed APIs	Subscription of APIs	Corporates
Aggregators	Unifying Rails/Stacks	Compare APIs	Ecommerce Companies
Backend Processors	Other Solutions APIs	Test APIs	BFSI Firms
Country Stacks	Workflow solutions	API Documentation	Other Providers
Content Providers	Value-added solutions	API Support	
Other Solution Providers		Configuration Handling	
		API Management	

3. Solutions Whose APIs Will Be Available in FAM

API providers across different products and solutions will be a part of FAM. They will offer solutions across Transactions, Data, Analytics, Risk, Operations, Customer Service and Value Adds. Broadly they can be classified under:

a. **Multi Stacks** – These are players who would offer complete end to end solution either across Multiple Fintech segments of specific segment involving combinations of various APIs from above categories. These combinations can be across various packages for e.g. Basic, Medium and Advanced. These packages will be largely based on Popular combinations, Transaction Volumes, Features and Pricing. So, user firms can simply pick a package based on licence or approval and quickly launch their solution. These are usually whitelabled SAAS (Software as a service) providers. Some examples are a complete payment stack, Neo Banking stack, etc.

b. **Custom Stacks** – Firms which want to create their own stack and not subscribe to standardized packages, or want some specific set of APIs only for embedding into their solutions, will go for Custom Stack. They can compare APIs in a particular category and choose to create various combinations of APIs needed to build their solution.

i. **Core Solutions** – This will consist of solutions like Core Banking, ERP, CRM, Workflow tools, Hosting/Cloud, Data and Mapping Solutions. These will concern the core activities of the Fintech. There can be complete stacks provided by a core player.

ii. **Product Focussed solutions** – This will cover APIs specific to areas like Loans, Deposits, Payments, Wealth Management, Insurance, Banking, Cards, Wallets, etc.

iii. **Unifying Stacks/Rails** – This covers various tech stacks and backbone infrastructure created across respective countries covering areas like Identity, Tax, E-governance, Authentication, Certification, Consent, Data sharing, Data aggregation, Interoperability/Portability etc. These will largely focus on creating trust in the system (like Unifying, Standardizing, Licencing, Certifying, authenticating, etc.), and linking with Govt. Services/activities. Like India has created AADHAR (For Identity and Authentication), UPI (Unified Payment rail), PSD2 and Open Banking in Europe and UK respectively.

iv. **Other Solutions** – This will cover a range of solutions either supporting, enabling the above or value-added solutions viz. Social Media, Communication Solutions viz. Chatbots etc., Content APIs, Loyalty and Rewards, Gamification APIs, Aggregation, Financial Planning, Other tools viz. Robotics, OCR, Analytics, Reporting, etc.

Based on all the above APIs, user firms will create central database engine, rules/logic for respective layers (as defined in FLARE), embed the APIs across various workflows and extend these to users over a frontend interface.

4. FAM Users

New or existing firms viz. Financial Services Firms, Fintechs, Start-up's, SME's, Corporates, Institutions or even Individuals can visit FAM, to create their solutions ground up, or to embed APIs as part of their platform.

Some Solution Providers in FAM can be users too, as they can purchase and integrate additional APIs, for value addition of their existing offerings.

There can be a new set of players, who will come to FAM and improve upon an existing API or merge/aggregate few APIs (to solve a problem by unifying use cases or simplifying a process). So, while they will consume some core APIs from marketplace, they will also publish these improvised APIs or combinations for others to choose from.

They will simply visit FAM, and once they identify themselves and their needs, they will be suggested various APIs, with use cases and Indicative pricing (Base, Per transaction and periodic, if any). They can then compare, also read feedback, access some usage/performance statistics for these APIs, etc. They will then select and purchase the APIs/solutions, there will be ability to try/test/validate, do single point onboarding with all selected solution vendors/providers, manage subscriptions, configure and quickly go live.

The users will thereby benefit in terms of:

a. FAM will enable anyone to start a Fintech (as long as they fulfil regulatory criteria)

b. Faster go to market – from concept to launch
c. Faster product enhancements, new feature additions
d. Better control and Big Savings on cost and time
e. Focus more on relationship and service, rather than tech and product
f. Easier to replace Solution, if service not good
g. Low Capex and Variable Opex to better manage costs

5. Features and Capabilities of FAM

Following are the features and capabilities that FAM will provide, to ensure its true potential is realized by users:

a. **Single Point Onboarding** for Both Solution Provider and Users, thereby eliminating a lot of efforts on either side. This will require due diligence/KYC to be done on players/users, collecting and validating requisite documentation, approvals/licences, certifications, risk assessment in terms of Financial Strength, operational strength assessing providers background and reliability etc. This single point Onboarding will eliminate the need for either supplier/vendor or User to Onboard each other. At best they will access data from the Marketplace about each other and fulfil some offline procedures to sign an agreement.

b. **Categorized and Tagged APIs** based on Use Cases and Needs. We have already indicated earlier, on what these categories will be. So, a wider option will ensure better suitability and acceptance and usage of FAM's. We expect a taxonomy will evolve across FAM, and help standardize various APIs with mappings to respective use cases.

c. Ability to **compare and select the APIs** based on parameters like price, features, usage statistics, user feedback etc. and proceed to Purchase

Note: API Pricing can be Pay per use, business volumes, slabwise, etc. This is an issue today, as people get charged for failed APIs in a pay per use model. So, this has to evolve. You can add APIs to cart and it will tell you approx. transaction cost at API level.

d. Relevant **documentation and Video's on the APIs** and how they can be used

e. To **Configure and Test the APIs** and eventually integrating them with User Journeys/workflows. Availability of preconfigured sets of APIs will hasten this process.

f. Defining and **configuring frontend features and personalization** based on Interfaces planned.

g. **Go Live and Publish** Your Solution Across Various Interfaces.

h. On an ongoing basis, FAM's will need to:

   i. Keep checking on availability of different APIs, and ensure they are not redundant but live.

   ii. Ensure reliability of APIs by tracking their success/failure rates.

   iii. Have better response times. Usually volume testing and ensuring proper hosting/connectivity enables better response time. So, this needs to be monitored and regularly fine tuned.

iv. An effective Orchestration of all APIs to ensure that they perform simultaneously or sequentially (as called for), to ensure the execution of a complete user flow.

v. Ensure appropriate security of APIs such that there is no unauthorized access, vulnerabilities or denial of services.

vi. Support services

i. Finally, FAM's need to enable the ability to quickly switch between providers i.e. API Portability. Again, standardization here will help.

Given the above capabilities in FAM, we expect that simple capabilities like embedding a product (Like payment API, KYC, API, etc.) to an existing solution, may be done in few minutes to few hours. Starting a new payment firm or wealth platform etc. should be done in matter of days, and finally launching a full stack Fintech or digital bank in matter of days to few weeks.

6. Other Enabling Aspects for FAM
a. Partnerships

Partnerships will be a very crucial driver in Fintech, and relationships between players will move from being Vendor or Service provider as it exists today, to a more partnership-based approach. There are few prime reasons why this will happen as explained below:

i. One is that because of APIs, many players will get more interconnected with each other

ii. Second, they will be on a similar platform (viz. cloud).

iii. Third, since most companies are moving from a Capex to a more Opex driven cycle, the financial binding between partners will be deeper, as success of one is connected with continuous success of other.

iv. Fourth aspect is they will share customers amongst themselves and also enable each other for new customer and business.

You can have partnerships at various levels for Fintech viz. Technology, Product, Service, Distribution or a mix of those. However, Technology will become core to all relationships, especially since they will be driven by FAM. Partnerships are also relevant as they enable innovation and create differentiation in offerings to clients.

Partners will be across various tiers, just like how it happens in Auto Industry. This will depend on how core is partner's solution to your overall offering. These tiers can be Tier 1 (Core Solutions), Tier 2 (Allied Solutions), Tier 3 (value adds), etc.

b. Sandbox for New Product Development, Testing and Go To Market

Sandboxes are replicated/simulated environments, which enable testing of new products or solutions in near live scenarios. They are very relevant, as Fintech is a highly regulated space and the cost of failures can be high. There may also be operational and technical risks associated, while introducing a new solution in a live environment. So, besides facilitating regulatory validation, Sandboxes also make available many plugins/technical/API connections related to the ecosystem, and possibly also data points and masters. To a great extent Sandboxes reduce time to validate and test a concept and accelerate go to market.

Sandboxes can be enabled by regulators, leading BFSI or Tech Firms may also create Sandboxes. We also see a good fitment for FAM's to have their own Sandboxes. So, FAM can thereby offer Sandbox features to Startups, and this will also do away with the need for extensive proof of concept projects (POC's) with Pilot customers, which Startups spend their efforts and resources on.

7. Sample Use Cases for FAM

We had mentioned that FAM can be used by various types of users to create a new solution or simply embed financial solution as part of their existing platform. These users are across categories, viz.

- Users like Individuals, Professionals, etc.
- Corporates, Institutions like colleges, Associations, Startups, SME's, etc. These people will offer Fintech solutions as part of their platform, which will be used within their closed ecosystem of Employees, students, members, vendors, etc.
- Neo Banks, Wealth Platforms, etc.

To better understand with some visualization on how this can be done, we present an example of a **College/University,** and how they can use FAM.

A College/University has various activities (Online and offline) and users as part of its ecosystem viz. Lectures, examination, events, certifications, training, administration across staff, professors, experts, canteen, hostel, external agencies (like affiliated university), auditors etc. One needs Fintech related solutions like Bank accounts, payments, loans, cards, QR code etc. for commercial conduct of the activities. Many other capabilities for core accounting, onboarding, community, events, user profiles, campus news, communication tools like email/chat, workflow solutions to support core activities, are also required. Many conduct their activities through their online portal/intranet which they get developed. However, with FAM, they can simply create a complete platform, and enable users in their ecosystem to conduct their respective activities. We have created few Stages and screens as below, which help us visualize the progression.

Stage 1 – Select the organization type. Based on the same, certain options will come (as can be seen below). Accordingly, the user will select the options.

Note: If the user wanted to just embed some capability in his existing platform then he would have selected Select own API.

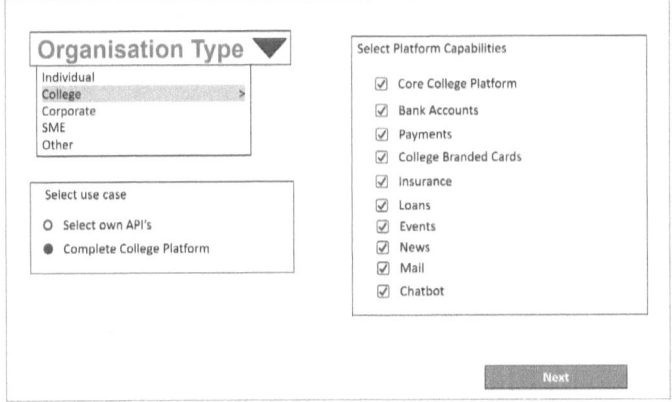

Stage 2 – Based on the functionalities selected in Stage 1, various solution option or API will be shown under respective categories. User can compare, see details (Documentation, Pricing, Features, User Reviews, Statistics, etc.) and accordingly select the concerned solution or API. The FAM will also mark these APIs as, Suggested, Popular, Low cost options, etc. to enable user to make choice. This can be based on some parameters. Once the set of solutions/APIs have been selected, user will move to Stage 3.

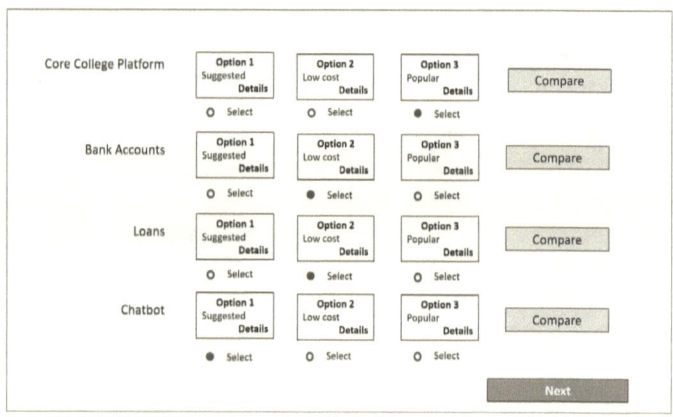

Stage 3 – This is a Stage where user will finalize and test the solution and make payment. Then he will proceed to Onboard, where certain documentation and user identity related formalities will be completed. As mentioned earlier, onboarding can be common across all solutions. Then comes Configure stage, where some technical details related to solution will be shared/specified. Post this is the workflow stage where specific workflows will be configured or tweaked (in case preconfigured workflow exists). We have illustrated under Activity Engine Layer in FLARE, on how the Workflow is configured and how various APIs get consumed. Then we have a Personalize stage, where one can provide personalization for look-n-feel and preview the solution. Once all is OK, one can publish the solution.

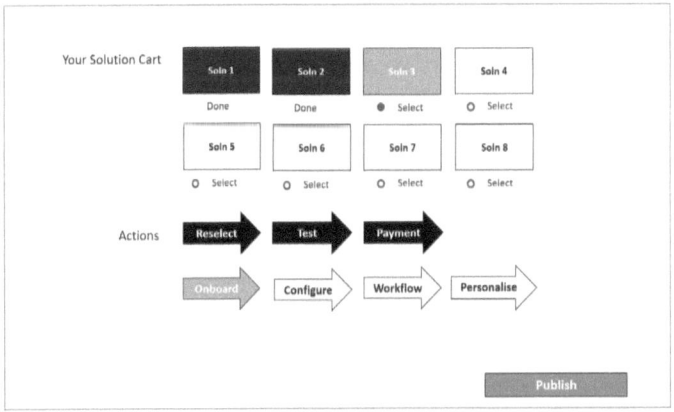

So, given the use case of College, we encourage readers to do the following:

- Identify a use case, and create your own Stagewise Illustration (Wireframe), of how it will be manifest through FAM.
- You can also create a Post Publish visualisation of the end solution, in a portal or mobile app form.
- Also, feel free to share your feedback and insights on FLARE by mailing at futurefintechframework@gmail.com

Other Key Aspects In Fintech

SECTION 03

OTHER KEY ASPECTS IN FINTECH

We have till now gone through some key themes and trends in Fintech in Section 1. Section 2 was all about 3F – Future Fintech Framework which enables us with a framework to apply these ideas and create innovative Fintech solutions. However, as Fintech Professionals we need to also be aware of few more key aspects, from a business and Fintech ecosystem perspective. These additional **Key aspects in Fintech** are:

A. **Fintech Players – Current and Emerging**
B. **Changing Income, Cost and Pricing Paradigm**
C. **Regulation and Compliance**
D. **Emergence of new roles/Career Opportunities**

Knowledge on the above aspects will help us to better understand the Fintech ecosystem and align to regulations, business and career opportunities. So, let us look at these key aspects in more details.

– A –

FINTECH PLAYERS – CURRENT AND EMERGING

We have understood and discussed various aspects about evolution of Fintech in Future. It therefore becomes imperative to discuss as to how the existing players and new ones will shape up in future. This is important, as we can get an overview of the likely structure and classification of Fintech players, and accordingly can visualize and plan based on how the ecosystem shapes up. So, let us look at some of these.

1. Current Key Players and Changing Landscape

Players Categories	Examples and Description	How They Are Changing
Financial Regulators	Regulating various Manufacturers, Networks, Distributors and Enablers in Fintech	They will increasingly see Automation at various levels especially in Regulatory, supervisory tech covering Monitoring, Compliance, Reporting, Penal Action and related areas. They will be proactive and lead innovation in many areas as we have discussed in relevant section of this book.
Licenced Manufacturers	Viz. Banks, Lending Companies, Payment Companies, Asset Management firms, Investment Advisors, Wealth Management, Insurance Companies, Stock Exchanges, Depositories, Pension Funds etc.	Enabling and creating Innovative products and solutions as per their assigned segments, Digitizing and Automation of Data, Transactions, Analytics to enable Onboarding, Risk Management, Advisory and Execution (Buy and Sale) of these. They are gradually also creating technology platforms for their products, and extending the same to their Distributors and customers, just like technology companies.

Players Categories	Examples and Description	How They Are Changing
Authorized Distributors	These are agencies like Direct Sales Agents (DSA's), IFA's, Corporate Agents, Brokers who enable distribution and sale of products and solutions from manufacturers	Lot of action happening here concerning tech integration and enablement of digital channels for Faster onboarding, focussed research, customized advisory and smart execution. Many platforms and backend tools are getting enabled for these intermediaries. Many Neo Banks, Robot Advisor players etc. are distributors/agents of licenced entities.
Networks Enablers	e.g. Swift (Global) and country wise networks like NEFT and RTGS (India), BACS (UK), ACH (US), RTGS (Many countries), Clearing Houses, Depositories etc.	They are offering value adds in reconciliation, operational risks, analytics. New players are emerging here with better product, services and use of technology like Blockchain. There is a move towards interconnectivity and standardization as that solves a lot of challenges in movement of funds.

Players Categories	Examples and Description	How They Are Changing
Card Networks	For e.g. Rupay, Mastercard, Visa, UnionPay, Amex etc.	These are automating and Enabling value adds like Remittances, Analytics, Better security services, Tokenisation, etc. We are seeing cards getting more integrated with lending/EMI's, enabling various form factors and capabilities like QR Codes, Biometrics, Mobile, Tap and Pay, etc.
Other Agencies	Like Credit Bureaus, Credit Rating Agencies, specialized agencies in collections, survey, valuations, Legal, Registrar and Transfer Agents etc.	They are improving their product range and automating operations, data, analytics, processing and interfaces with partners/customers, they offer their services to.
Technology Firms	Providing Technology applications for Above	They have made their services modular and offering Cloud and API-based solutions. These consist of easy to configure solutions with various channels and interfaces, for faster integration with other solutions etc. They are basically creating a plug and play platform for faster go to market and ease of management.

2. Emerging and Future Players

Player	Description
Aggregators	We are seeing aggregators emerging in areas like payments, Insurance, Mutual Funds, Loans, Trading, etc. These aggregators work across Data and Analytics which enable us to evaluate and compare products and solutions and many of these aggregators also enable transactions through API integration.
Robo Advisors	These are automated Investment solutions enabling digital onboarding, client profiling and risk assessment, portfolio allocation, rebalancing based on strategy or goals. They can also transact. Many robos are distributors/agents and are enabled by aggregators, networks and tech providers.
Digital Wallets	Wallets are a new form of digital payment solution which can be funded (like a prepaid card) and used for various forms of payment. These are usually mobile app driven and range from being open loop to closed loop, depending on how easy it is to move money around, and range of options they can be used for.

Player	Description
Ecommerce Players	Many non-financial players largely from ecommerce space have entered the Fintech segment as they have enabling synergies largely in areas like Payments and Lending. So, they have **embedded** various products as part of their platform, for Customers and Distributors on their ecommerce platform. The underlying financial product is usually an arrangement with some existing Fintech player. **Note:** If enabled by regulations these Fintech players can be sister concerns of the ecommerce players. Say a digital wallet.
Big Tech Players	Many big tech players like Google are also entering Fintech space. Just like Ecommerce Players, they are largely in areas like Payments and lending. In future, we feel that Big tech players can also play role in Identity and onboarding.
Community-Based Platforms	Apps offering Crowdfunding and P2P capabilities are emerging. These can be across Lending and Insurance and going forward these solutions will consolidate further. Many social media app-based companies will also enter this space.

Player	Description
Blockchain and Cryptocurrency Players	Leveraging the network and security strength of Blockchain, we see many consortiums emerge in areas like Trade Finance, Cross border settlement/payments and also various cryptocurrencies.
Pay Later	A new category of Payment option enabling customers to pay later (either lumpsum or in easy instalments) during checkout. This has expanded affordability and seen great adoption for online payments in ecommerce.
Assurance Products	We will see emergence of many products and services across Validation, Verification and Facilitation built around existing Fintech Solutions. So, something like Product and Provider Certification, Location Verification services, refund enablement and claims, Individual Credit assessment.
Specialized Fintech Content Players	These players will specialize in offering different forms of content to improve awareness, educate and engage various participants.
Fintech API Marketplace (FAM)	We have already discussed in detail about FAM earlier as part of 3F and, how many existing players will morph into FAM's. FAM's will thereby revolutionize the way new Fintech products and solutions are rolled out in Future.

Note: Many of the players identified above can vary in their description depending on the country and regulatory classification, ecosystem and practices therein.

Having understood about evolution of existing and new players, let us also get some understanding on how some types of categorization is taking shape amongst players in the Fintech ecosystem.

3. Players getting classified as Front End, Middle Level, Core Provider and Balance Sheet Players

We will gradually see a new category of client facing (front end) players emerging, who will differentiate based on the mix of their solution, better look and feel, convenience, servicing, pricing, Loyalty and relationship with clients. These players will go to a FAM and select appropriate APIs (individually or in preconfigured combinations) to create their solution.

Then there will be middle level players, who will provide services like reconciliation, processing, call centres, Operations services and Support, etc.

At the backend there will be core service providers, and they will focus more on core products, related apps, technology and infrastructure aimed at supporting themselves or frontend players. These will largely be Technology players or large Tech savvy Financial Firms. They will extend the Core or the Middle layers as whitelabled Stacks for 3rd parties to offer customer facing solutions, like we see in case of some Neo Banks.

Another aspect is that these players especially at Middle Layer and Core Layers will offer either Technology or Services or Both.

We also foresee that the core part of finance which is the Balance Sheet will be run and managed by specialists in Portfolio Management, ALM, Risk Management and Compliance. They will fund the frontend players, who will put together a tech platform, get funds from balance sheet players, to conduct business by acquiring and managing clients.

In a way, the front end is the Relationship layer (More of Business risk), Middle level provider is largely services (Operational Risk), Core Provider is usually the tech (mainly Technology Risk) and Balance Sheet Provider (More of Financial Risk).

4. Focused Segment and Product Based Solutions

Another trend we can see is that many Fintech's are targeting specialized segments or product categories viz.

- a. **Segments** – Small and Medium Businesses, Millennials, College Students, Travellers, Senior Citizens, Blue Collar workers, etc.
- b. **Products** – Travel Card, Salary Loans, Invoice Financing, Travel Insurance, Health Insurance, etc.

5. Both Unbundling and Bundling Happening

We will increasingly see that Players and segments will get unbundled, and eventually some form of Product/Solution gets bundled or packaged for customers.

Let us take an example of Lending, where, based on specialization, the processes/activities are getting unbundled and being bundled or packaged by frontend players.

So, activities like funding/balance sheet, marketing, client acquisition, Onboarding and KYC, Credit assessment of users, operations and customer services and finally Collection are getting unbundled. Each of these activities can be outsourced to external agencies, across both Technology platform and services. The company at the front end will manage these agencies, and put together an interesting package/value proposition for end users, ensure a level of service and experience for client. We can see this evolution in Automobile Industry too, where most parts in a car are actually built by external vendors. In some cases, even the engine of the car is from external vendors. So, the car company is just assembling and managing the solution/services for the customer, and they have outsourced all the other activities from other vendors/partners.

6. Partnership and Alliances

New forms of partnership and alliances will keep happening till we see some form of natural groupings emerge. While front end players and brands will compete with each other, many Core and Middle level Players will form Partnerships and Alliances and integrate with each other. We have already provided more details about Partnership as part of FAM, and also discussed the context under various sections in the book.

7. Other Key Players Enabling Fintech

Besides various players in Fintech as well as role played by regulators, it is important to discuss on the role played by Angel Funds, Venture Capital (VC) Funds as well as Incubators and Accelerators. While VC largely have been instrumental in funding great Fintech ideas and enabled them to partner and go to market, through their network. Incubators and accelerators have provided Fintechs with Physical and Technical Infrastructure to run their initial operations, key insights, mentoring, operational expertise and guidance, networking help, etc. In many places where the Incubator or Accelerators are driven by financial players themselves, Fintech firms have been also offered technical access to core systems and networks which helped the Fintechs build and test their product. As a next logical step, many of these Financial Players also became the Fintechs first customer too. These players will continue to play a very crucial role for growth of the Fintech ecosystem in Future too. In fact, adopting 3F – Future Fintech Framework will help them evaluate opportunities and ensure that the Fintechs they work with can be more successful.

–B–

CHANGING INCOME, COST AND PRICING PARADIGM

Given new business models, Players, Product and solutions in Fintech, we have also seen emergence of new types of income, charges and approach to pricing. This has changed the revenue mix of Financial Services firms too. Till recently, Financial services including Banks depended on Income largely from:

1. Spread
2. Float
3. Transaction Charges and Brokerage
4. Asset Based Charges (AMC)
5. Premiums
6. Commissions
7. Other fees and Charges

Spread (i.e. the difference between Interest Received and Interest Paid) was usually predominant, followed by Float and transaction charges. Other fees were not such significant. But with computerization, retail expansion, some level of automation in payments and competition, there has been some changes in this revenue mix. With Float almost vanishing and Spread vastly reducing, the proportion of income from transaction fees and charges have increased. Many resorted to Cross sell of 3rd party products, and this also resulted in increase in Commissions and Brokerages.

To shore up revenues through other fees and charges, we have already seen banks and financial firms levying Minimum balance charges, in cards we have seen annual subscription charges, charges on ATMs, Debit Card Issuance Charges, etc. Similarly, in Wealth Management, Investments, Insurance and other segments, we see changes in the revenue mix. We feel this trend will continue for some more time. So, with unbundling amongst players, partnerships and new Fintech segments, a vast variety of new income streams, levies and charges will emerge. So, let's look at some of the recent changes, and also explore some of the expanded Avenues for Income, Cost and Pricing as below:

1. **API Charges** – Since, tech solutions and platforms have been added to their offerings, Banks and Fintech firms will levy charges on parties who will use (consume) their APIs. Currently APIs are either free or they are charged on basis of Calls. Each request is a call and then there is a response to that request. However, call-based API charges have

their drawbacks as you get charged for failed API requests (where there is no response). We expect this will change to Slab wise charges, based on number of transactions, or an annual charge being levied on the same. There can be clauses and penalties too based on Failure rates. This will become a big source of revenue going forward for Fintechs.

2. **Privilege based charges** – These charges will be based on certain privileges like better and faster services, customized solutions, etc.

3. **AUM/Asset Handling fees** – We already know of such a charge in Wealth/Investment space, but this will also start getting levied in other segments including Bank accounts. We already see trends of Negative interest rate being levied; this is like some form of maintenance charge for balance in your account. Though this is just an analogy, as the move towards negative interest rate is a larger economic process. The intent is to challenge traditional thinking and highlighting similarities in the difference.

4. **Interchange Fees** – Interchange is largely a charge levied when a transaction usually originates or is routed through a third-party network. We see this in ATMs, i.e., if you withdraw from a 3rd party ATM, then there is some interchange charge exchanged between your bank/card and 3rd party (to whom ATM belongs). With partnerships, we can see this

category of charge increasing. Though, Banks and Fintech firms may decide to either charge the customer or make it free.

5. **Data-based Charges** – There is a possibility of certain charges being levied based on amount of Data provided/shared. This will however be subject to Data privacy and security norms. This is key in future, as there is a reason for the saying, that data is the new oil. We can for example have separate pricing based on data/information shared while taking a loan. Another example is, if an individual agrees to share/reveal certain type of data, some charges are waived off and many more possibilities. Regulations permitting, Fintech firms may simply make money by monetizing and sharing the data with concerned 3rd parties. So, keep tuned to this possibility.

6. **Platform fees** – Fintech firms may levy fees for usage of a value-added platform, say for corporates or Robo Advisory. This can be something like an annual charge or charges on number of users, etc.

7. **Foreign Exchange Income** – Income from foreign exchange is a key source of income for card, travel and remittance-based products. Going forward though margins will be under pressure, we expect this may increase, as there is more global travel and also global ecommerce etc. We already see many business models built

around remittances, card-based products for travellers, etc.

8. **Subscription Fees** – In future, Fintech firms may sell you subscription-based services and generate income in the same way they sell third-party products. This can be for specialized and popular content or for specialized services.

9. **Income from Advertisements and Promotions** – There may be certain services which can be free in case customers are open for promotions. This opens up an avenue for Advertisement/promotion-based revenues.

10. **Customized Pricing** – Pricing may move from being product, solution, transaction driven to being customized as per Customer's Profile, share of wallet and/or usage. Aspects like Life Time Value (LTV) will have big impact on determining pricing for client. So, same product will be priced differently for different customers or categories. This approach will completely change the dynamics of revenue mix or income predictability, and its success will be largely determined by having a large number of loyal long-term customers.

11. **Incentives and Discounts** – We will see more of incentives and discounts being offered to customers for referrals. So, if a customer is an influencer and is responsible for retaining and/or getting many new customers, then such influencers will be rewarded. Similarly,

there is also large emphasis on Incentives for employees, agents and distributors.

12. **Income from Research and Advisory** – This stream will also pick up, as regulations are beginning to distinguish firms, based on Transactions and Advisory capabilities. Usually research and advisory based income is determined by Asset being handled, performance based or even flat subscription charge.

13. **Capital Expenditure (Capex) to Operating Expenses (Opex)** – Currently many incumbent financial firms face a large amount of Capex (Investment in Premises, hardware, software etc,). However, with Fintech's resorting to completely Digital offerings, Cloud and Advent of APIs, they will all likely move to a pay as you use (Opex) model. This implies, there is either negligible or zero initial fixed costs (Capex). So, in future many Fintech business models are more likely to be based on Opex. This will accelerate as unbundling happens, where the Balance sheet play is separated from Tech and Operations for Fintech. Even capital intensive activities in ATMs and PoS will move from Capex to Opex. We already see this happening.

14. **Usage based charges** – Another trend that is emerging is that you pay as you use. This is especially true for Products like Insurance, credit, etc.

15. **Penalties and Fines** – Firms may also resort to charging penalties and fines for any deficiency in commitment from clients. This will be in a way extension of charges like late payment, fees, missed payments, not maintaining minimum balance, unable to meet some obligations on time, not intimating/communicating, etc.

Note: The above aspects will however be subject to Privacy norms and regulations. Also, relevance of many aspects will depend on the Product or Segment.

We have seen many Fintech firms falter while pricing, by attempting innovative approach to garner market share, and even offering their products and solutions for free. This is not sustainable and Fintech firms will need to look at Unit Economics, Transaction wise costs, trends, volumes and profitability before deciding on their Income, Costs and Pricing mix. Therefore, it is important to get a picture of different metrics involved, as it will help us to innovatively work out the best Income, Costs or Pricing mix. Eventually, sustained commercial success will only be determined, by the way Fintech firms price their solutions and generate revenues on one hand, and on the other hand, how they manage costs and risk in Fintech.

–C–

REGULATION AND COMPLIANCE

Financial Sector is a highly regulated Industry. In various countries there are multiple agencies, which are creating enabling ecosystems to accelerate new product development, or enhancing existing offerings in Fintech. These can be in nature of new licensed entity types which are into Identity enablement, account aggregation, open banking, backend processing and reconciliation etc. Besides, given the changing Fintech ecosystem, aspects like privacy, safety and services related regulations are being looked into, or getting redefined by regulators. The main aim is to retain trust, improve efficiency, reduce risk in the system, and enhance offerings for the end consumers, by leveraging technology.

Therefore, moving forward we highlight some key aspects pertaining to regulations and compliance, which will gain prominence and need to be looked out for, given evolution of Fintech.

1. **Privacy and Data protection** – With lots of data being generated and captured in the

digital economy (including Fintech), the right use and handling of data becomes important. We will therefore have to be aligned with many Privacy and Data regulations (Enacted or in Process) across various countries, usually covering aspects like:

- Classification of types of data, their handling and treatment
- How data need to be stored and processed, including encryption and anonymized data
- Taking consent of users while gathering/capturing data
- Defining purpose of use of data, and what will be misuse
- Sharing of data within and with 3rd parties – what is allowed and what is not
- Monetization of the data
- Deletion of Data, etc.

Note: We have already seen this trend beginning with GDPR in Europe. Besides, this aspect becomes more complex in scenarios where there is partnership, use of social media, collaboration and integration between various entities to acquire, service and manage clients. So, it will be important to identify who will own the data, store the data, process the data and related responsibilities.

2. **Cybersecurity** – With more and more digital channels and devices in place, the whole gamut of cyber security is very important, especially given the high propensity of frauds and security breaches in Fintech. So, we can see increasing involvement of Regulators in areas like security validations and certifications of systems, processes applications, monitoring and reporting, encryptions to be followed and other technical guidelines in Data, cloud, related security measures etc. We already see certain guidelines concerning using different types of user authentication, caching, masking, using https, encryption of data during transfer and storage, not to keep unwanted ports open, securing endpoints etc. With complexity of technology, these guidelines will get better defined and refined. There can also be related guidelines on Certification, education, user awareness, warning, alert and/or notification.

3. **New segments and Licencing policies** – Given evolving technology, ecosystem, Business Models, user needs etc., regulators will increasingly look at new segments of business like they have done in recent past about Aggregators, Payment Networks, New generation digital only providers like neo banks, Open Banking, Wallets, etc. Not just that, regulators are also at forefront to propel usage of technologies like Cloud, Blockchain,

IoT and Social Media. So, we may see new segments emerging and licencing in regards to the same. For example, in line with 3F, we may see new licences/entities being authorized as Fintech Marketplaces (part of FAM). The regulations for these marketplaces will talk about policies and guidelines for technical distribution of Fintech Related APIs and aspects like Onboarding, security, business continuity, etc.

4. **Risk Norms** – Given the dynamic nature of a technology driven Fintech ecosystem, their integration and interdependence between players, Regulators will be more dynamic and proactive on aspects like Capital, Provisioning, Margining, Special Fund/pool, other transaction charges etc., aimed at creating a more level playing field for smaller players. There may also be norms specified towards Layering of risk, pooling and netting off etc. to make risk provisioning both sufficient and efficient. In an increasingly digital ecosystem, aspects like multiplier effect, domino effect, interdependence of players, layers of risk, velocity of money etc. need to be also well understood, defined or redefined in the digital Fintech space.

5. **Segregation of players** – We have already discussed, about the possibility that, Balance sheet (Finance) part of the Fintech business

gets segregated from Technology, Operations, processing and other front-end activities (involving acquiring and managing customers) in Fintech. This will ensure the Financial Risk aspect is left to robust players. So, there may be enabling regulations and policies by regulators, encouraging such segregation to happen.

6. **Automated Audits** – We are increasingly going to see automated audits and reporting by regulators. These audits will go beyond financial audits and involve Marketing, Transaction, Process, Security and Technology Audits too. Accordingly, various red flags will be raised and probably some form of ratings assigned to Fintech firms concerning various risks and breaches. This needs to be however differentiated from customer risk assessment or transaction monitoring about Money Laundering, frauds etc. There shall also be regulations and reporting on app level audits to be performed.

7. **User level training, certification and/or Licencing** – Regulators may specify industry bodies/quasi regulatory agencies, who will manage the training, certification/licencing of these users/firms. Infrastructure for this already exist. With Fintech, this segment will accelerate, as education and awareness, is the best way to enable regulations, fill knowledge gaps and gain trust of end users.

8. **Pricing, Promotion and Mis-selling** – In the Fintech world we can see a lot of incentives, freebies aimed at onboarding and retaining the client. Many times, Fintechs go overboard on these client acquisition drives/marketing expenses, to the extent that it does not make any financially viable case. Besides, we have seen a lot of mis-selling (through improper communication, incentives, etc.) and false promises being made to users. We therefore foresee that Regulators, will increasingly step in (either directly or indirectly) to curb such improper promotion (which disrupts the economics and defies conventional business logic, makes false promises or is improperly worded to create a wrong impression with customers), Mis-selling, Predatory Pricing and even profiteering as a result. It is not just about such pricing with new customers, but transparency in pricing for existing customers is also a concern. We have seen multiple cases on the aspects highlighted here and regulators may end up providing some guidelines to curb any practices that take advantage of the customer.

9. **Product and Service Deficiency** – Regulations will also increasingly focus on service and product related performance and deficiencies. There can be guidelines that specify some benchmarks about Service levels and

Turnaround time (TAT) for Customer Service, Processing, Resolutions, Refunds, Reporting and Transparency. There is also a need for some balance in resource allocation between client acquisition and servicing efforts, as it is more skewed to client acquisition. So, regulators may specify some ratio to be maintained towards dedicated client servicing resources, as this is a big gap not just in Fintech but overall, in financial services. There should be penalties and action both for individual level breach and also at aggregate levels.

10. **Client Redressal** – There is a serious need for a framework for quick escalation, redressal, reimbursement to customers as this process is currently not very transparent and effective. A charter with respective contacts and escalation matrix needs to be enforced, rather than a non-transparent, bureaucratic and anonymized process which exists now. Also, these client metrics should be tracked and rated at regulator level with corrective and punitive action on the players as needed. Such measures are more important to be clearly defined by regulators, especially with low touch Digital only offerings.

11. **Rationalization and Convergence** – There can be some form of rationalization and convergence amongst regulators in areas like, a form of common certification for shared/common entities, unified KYC guidelines,

simplified reporting, flexibility in operations (remove repeats, plug gaps while removing overlaps).

12. **API Guidelines** – With the next generation of Fintech driven largely by API economy, the issues of API ownership and responsibility needs to be fixed from a regulatory perspective. Even guidelines about API standardization, availability, uptime, response time/performance and pricing of APIs needs to be broadly defined, to ensure that there is service availability, continuity and there are no wrongful practices.

13. **Misuse of technology** – We will also see regulations aimed at stopping misuse of technologies like AI and IoT against end customers.

It is not that regulators are not cognizant of the above. In fact, in many countries there are specific guidelines to address some of the above aspects, and these will undergo changes as ecosystem evolves. But the challenge for regulators and players will be to:

1. Find the right **balance between Regulations and Innovation**. This can happen by wider participation of players during formulation of regulations and a continuous feedback and faster improvement loop between regulators and players.

2. **Need to make regulations and compliance to work silently behind the screen, while ensuring they are simple, transparent and effective** – This is possible through Automation which is driven by AI and Analytics.

3. **Keep costs low** (in past we have seen regulations adding to cost) – We have increasingly seen that regulations and compliance have added to the costs, and made the processes complex for all. So, going forward in the new Fintech ecosystem, regulators need to be mindful of this metric while rolling out or amending new regulations, guidelines, policy etc. Here too Automation, rationalization and merger of processes and activities will help.

4. **Standardization and Differentiation** – There will be increasing pressure to standardize various activities, technologies and processes (especially with cost considerations), but again a balance needs to be found such that there is scope for creating differentiation by Fintech players. So, while we feel increasingly products and processes will get standardized. Players will differentiate through packaging, pricing, service types, personalization etc. and we can see this evolution in FAM too. This way regulators can better regulate the product/segment, while allowing freedom for market forces, and innovation by front-end players, without being intrusive.

5. Massively **Ramp up their Surveillance and Enforcement** – Currently, we see serious capacity constraints with Regulators, which compromises surveillance and timely punitive or corrective actions. Besides, recruiting more people, outsourcing this to self-regulatory bodies/agencies etc., regulatory bodies can also take help of Digitization and automation for a massive ramp up in capacity. With real time tech and processing, they need to move fast.

6. **Business Continuity** – While technology driven innovation ensures new products and solutions, we will also see many failures in Fintech (both at product level and organization level) because of business, financial or regulatory reasons. So, using automation we need to create early warning indicators, to take timely pre-emptive or corrective action for business continuity. It is important to note that having a proper ecosystem with portability, standardized APIs, simplified onboarding practices and tech guidelines from Regulators, are also important factors, for ensuring business continuity. These ensure that clients can be quickly switched and ported to new provider, if one fails.

7. **To be preventive, corrective or Punitive and not just disruptive** – Too much regulatory disruption, inaction or gradual action has been detrimental to lots of business models and players. We need to have clear guidelines,

and not leave grey areas which are open for multiple interpretations. Besides, guidelines should not frequently be tweaked in a big way, and adhoc, knee jerk policies must be avoided. Such regulatory disruption is not healthy, and adds to the cost and even detrimental to end consumer at times (whom the regulator wishes to safeguard).

8. **Deputed Responsible Authority (DRA)** – Today there are authorities/and departments within a financial firm/Fintechs, which look after regulation and compliances. The only problem is that these departments and employees are working for and getting paid by the Financial Firms. Because of this conflict of interest, though many problems/issues are known, but effective, timely and corrective actions are not taken. We strongly feel there is a need to have DRA, who will work with Financial firms/Fintech players on specific compliance roles, but get paid and be employee of the regulators. Regulators can in turn charge the Financial firms for DRA's assigned to them. This can be for crucial roles, as identified by regulators and since they work and report to regulators, they are not burdened by a firm's internal dynamics, hierarchy and vested interests. DRA's won't add to cost (as it is just transfer from one entity to another), but can make a difference to curb regulations

and compliance related deviations in industry. This is different than Auditors who are more occasional.

9. **Level Playing field** – Regulators need to increasingly ensure better level playing field amongst players and prevent predatory pricing, misuse of dominant position/market share by players. So, increasingly regulators will step in to define these critical parameters and respective red flags for each of them.

10. **Coordination between Regulators** – Given global nature of commerce and Fintech, we will increasingly see more cooperation and collaboration between regulators within a country, and amongst countries, and this can begin with Payments. There can be country to country collaboration or regional cooperation like SEPA in Europe. This will increase efficiencies of payments transfer, reduce risk (and related costs) including in areas like money laundering. Industry associations and platforms can also play a role in this.

So, we now have a good overview of many aspects and challenges concerning Regulations and Regulators. Either the regulations will lead (Regulator driven Innovation) or they will catch up, and this is bound to have an impact on Process, Technology, Risks and costs and therefore important to be mindful of as a Fintech Professional.

–D–

EMERGENCE OF NEW ROLES/ CAREER OPPORTUNITIES

By now, we have understood various Fintech themes and how they can be overlaid across the 3F components viz. FDLC, FLARE and FAM, to foster innovation in Digital Fintech space. We now move on to another key aspect i.e. understand various roles and career opportunities that will emerge or gain prominence as part of evolving Fintech landscape, as proposed in 3F Framework. This understanding is important, as it enables students and Professionals aspiring for a career in Fintech, to orient and train themselves accordingly. Corporate and HR departments in Fintech and related firms can also look into these roles and related insights, to plan recruitment, training and career paths for their employees.

Currently a lot of activities in Fintech is being entrusted/facilitated through roles like Product Managers, Project Managers, Business Analysts, Domain Experts, UI and UX Experts, Digital Marketing experts etc. While these roles will continue to be in demand, we feel that some of the existing role will gain prominence and new roles will emerge as below:

1. **Community Managers** – Community has already been highlighted as a crucial Fintech theme. In FDLC, we have also discussed about how a community driven approach will gain prominence for Acquiring and engaging with prospects and customers. All this will require a specialized role of Community Managers who will plan and manage the engagement initiatives with a particular community. These community managers will thereby help in defining product features, pricing, communications and content, aimed at engaging and deepening relationship with clients. In fact, you can see this trend across Fintechs where products and solutions are targeted at a particular niche/segment say SME's, College Students, Young Professionals, Citizens Overseas, etc. They will also help is surveys, various campaigns and events, to better understand and regularly engage with the community. Community-based approach also complements influencer marketing and improves loyalty, engagement and profitability for Fintech firms. Community managers will help track the influencers, build community calendars, coordinate events, etc. These Managers will also look at profitability, market share from perspective of the community. They will also help maintain relationships

with respective community associations and have skills and knowledge about the specific community. Alignment of product features, user experience/journey with specific community is also something they will work on along with product managers.

2. **Partnership Managers** – Partnerships and alliances will be key drivers both at Strategic levels and at Tactical levels. They can spread across Product, Process/operations, Business and/or Technology. In fact, be it a Vendor, Distributor or other types of partnerships, they will become more deeply embedded with each other.

At strategic levels the tie ups can be deeper, with firms offering complementing products and solutions. This will involve deeper technical and operational integration. At tactical level, the tie-up can be for simple referral programs, offers and discounts which is more ongoing and a campaign or promo driven arrangement. This can be managed through front-end integration and exchange of information.

So, besides market and business development skills, Partnership Managers need technical understanding, effective program management, negotiations, pricing skills too. These Partnership and Alliance managers will keep scouting for opportunities, and cast their net wide across participants in industry, through networking and industry events. They may even run campaigns aimed at getting new partners. These Managers will thereby scout, manage and align the partners in line with organizations strategy, operations and business goals.

3. **Loyalty Experts** – Loyalty experts will help design loyalty programs. These programs can be product specific, community, category or user specific. Along with Product, Marketing and Community Managers, they will design loyalty campaigns and programs aimed at deepening relationship with customers, communities and/or segments. They must carry good understanding of customer life stages, product and solution usage to improve LTV. They will also be complemented by other roles accordingly. Managing and tracking these campaigns will also be a part of their responsibility.

4. **Gamification Experts** – We have increasingly seen the importance of gamification and how it can be used to drive engagement, usage, transactions etc. across FDLC. In fact, Gamification superimposed on Loyalty, can be used to open up features, facilities and privileges to customers, based on life stages. Similarly, gamifications can be applied to campaigns, tools, events, actions and transactions too. All this depends on the level of planning and

resources made available. Gamification experts will need to thereby understand the various stages of customers journey in a product/solution, and how to Gamify them, make them interesting and engaging. The game theme, levels, rewards etc. will need to be conceptualized and embedded across respective journeys. They will also have a good understanding of different forms of gamification, and how it works with various customer categories, suitability across respective interfaces etc. Interaction with various stakeholders is also needed.

5. **User Journey experts** – These are UI and UX experts who will help design various journeys and interactions for a particular product, across users and segments. They will largely look at design cues to make the experience better for users and also suggest cues in regards to adding user/community specific capabilities like language, personalization (color, images, etc.). They will also look into areas like user surveys, usage analytics etc. Basically, completing the feedback loop, which enables them to keep refining, improving and updating the user journeys. This role is also key with emergence of Multiple interfaces and channels, where user initiates a request or transaction from one channel, engages over another channel and fulfilment is done through third channel. The key is to have convenient and intuitive

fulfilment, without any broken experience. They will work in coordination with Product teams, community and marketing teams to create and update respective journeys.

6. **Campaign Managers** – Campaign manager will be responsible for designing and managing various campaigns for different products and solutions, aimed at respective users/segments. These campaigns can of various types viz. promos, new offers/discounts, event based (both user level and community level), cross sell, up sell, awareness, education, etc. A mix of Marketing managers, content managers, product managers, community manager etc. will work alongwith the Campaign manager to make the campaigns effective. These will be measured on basis of reach, engagement and response.

7. **Event Managers** – Event managers will help organize and manage events specific to customer/segment. Again, just like campaigns these events can be specific to networking, awareness, relationship building, cross sell/upsell. User participation and response would be a good measure to track effectiveness of events.

8. **Content Managers** – By now, we have got a feel of what all is happening with Community, Loyalty, events, Campaigns, user journeys etc.. For engagement across all these activities

with users, we need good content. These contents can be across various mediums, channels, forms and languages. The content manager has to curate, categorize and facilitate provision of these content across various mediums. They shall coordinate with content providers either in-house or from outsourced specialist.

9. **Content Creators** – These will be specialists in creating different types of content. Some of them can be specialized based on type of content (viz. Video, Infographics, Banners), technical and domain knowledge-based content, and also experts with Language and Communication skills. Many of these involve activities like Newsletter, research reports, tutorials, snapshots/briefs etc. and may be outsourced based on expertise and sensitivity.

10. **Social Media Experts** – These are experts who will manage the engagement with users across various social media. The level of their activity will depend on how deeply is social media integrated, the level of strategy/resources dedicated etc. Currently many such activities are managed at a broader level and even outsourced. But as privacy and compliance aspects become stronger, we see this activity becoming more in-house. There will thereby be a need for dedicated teams in specific areas, and they may work in tandem with respective

community and marketing managers. For e.g. running a blog with continuous engagement and response to user interactions, and not just bot-based interventions.

11. **Regulations Experts** – We have mentioned that Privacy, Security and compliance aspects are gaining importance from a regulatory standpoint, and also addressed them across various Sections in 3F. But these regulation and framework needs to be ably supported by legal experts in these areas, as they are necessary in providing inputs for agreements, systems/ technology, Product, operations, transaction monitoring, risk and fraud management. They will thereby help at design level (i.e. when a new system, tech, product or solution is created), at operations level (guidelines to regularly manage deviations, exceptions, regulatory reporting, servicing, etc.), and to firefight, in case of any breach or problems. Today a lot of expertise needs to be built in these areas, as nuances of technology, products, channels, direct access and different user types have made the whole situation very complex. A lot of training needs to be done to create a knowledge base of professionals in these areas with the focus to enable business and not make it more challenging. These opportunities will not only emerge with Fintech Players, but also amongst regulators, as there will be need for employees

with experience in Onboarding, Managing, Monitoring and Audit the Participants.

12. **API Managers** – We have already discussed about the importance of APIs, and how they will enable new forms of collaborations, innovations, business models to accelerate growth in Fintech. Besides, we have also seen the challenges with API, and how they need to be effectively managed and monitored on an ongoing basis. It is this mix of opportunities and challenges that will give rise to the importance of API managers, who will have ownership of respective sets of APIs. These APIs can be grouped based on systems, products, domain/area, internal/external etc. and assigned to managers based on business need, expertise. The API manager will work towards making these APIs available, help in integration, tracking usage, uptimes, success rates, interacting with technical teams, consumers of these APIs, troubleshooting etc. In fact, for Fintech firms, APIs will become more important source of revenue. So, these managers will also help in pricing and monetization of these APIs, and also manage aspects like documentation, versions etc. Based on feedback, usage, industry needs, trends, new developments, etc., API Managers can initiate improvement, merger of existing APIs or development of new APIs, as the business

case may justify. This ownership of APIs is needed both for APIs Published and for APIs consumed. While for APIs consumed, Product managers with understanding of APIs may be able to manage. For Published APIs, the need of API Managers is specifically required.

13. **Data Experts** – With advent of new technologies, systems, user generated data, usage data, interaction between systems, Internet, real time analytics, voice, text, videos, etc., there is an increasing need to manage, curate, store, process and translate actionable insights from data. Hence, at various levels we need experts to manage this data. Thus, at one level there is need for **Data Analyst** to handle and perform tasks on this data. In the next level, we need **Data Engineers,** who will structure these data into logical, technical models, frameworks, cubes, relationships, tags, etc. This is as per the technology, data software in use, warehouse created. Another aspect of data pertains to Analytics, and that is where **Data Scientists** step in. Data scientists are more of an expert in data analytics, Statistics and related data models, than data itself. So, in absence of Data engineers and the base work they do to create and manage the data sets, Data Scientists can achieve little. This needs to be kept in mind as often many data analytics, ML or AI projects fail because of challenges with base data.

14. **Machine learning and Artificial Intelligence (ML and AI) experts** – Similar to Data Scientists, ML and AI experts depend on base data sets, which they use to create their respective data models. It is based on these data models that they run their respective ML/AI algorithms, to train the system and generate automated insights/recommendations/actions.

15. **Data Visualization and Reporting experts** – These are experts who specialize in various reporting tools, data visualization tools and techniques. They may supplement, complement the work done by data engineers or support data scientists. They will enable the best choice of visualization, presentation of data, based on the use case.

16. **Cloud Experts** – With growing importance of cloud and hosted solutions like SaaS, PaaS and IaaS, there is an increasing need for experts in Cloud. Their need will also be felt with increasing partnerships, and need of integration between players, who can be from different cloud sets.

17. **Process Experts** – With increasing use of new technologies and automations like RPA, AI and ML there is an increasing need for experts who can understand and translate these processes into these respective technologies. They need to thereby have good understanding of the processes and be trained in usage of respective

process automation tools. The aim is to process faster, reduce errors and control costs through use of process reengineering, technology and automation. They may be supported technically as required, or depending on complexity of tool involved.

18. **Knowledge Managers and Trainers** – A lot of knowledge and information is getting generated either through sources like regulations, industry actions, new products, technology, risk incidences, disputes, operational developments etc. This knowledge needs to be gathered, assimilated, stored, analyzed and converted into insights for Education, Awareness and training of different users, including customers. So, we expect an increasing engagement across Knowledge management, Training and awareness of users including customers. This role also becomes important, as in Fintech many aspects including training and certification can be driven by regulations.

Over the years, evolution of Banking, Financial services and Insurance (BFSI) Segment started with an emphasis on domain-based skills in Banking, Credit, Payments, Treasury, Investments, Insurance, etc. As gradual evolution and expansion happened with new branches and distribution channels, skills like branch management, distribution and Agent management were much sought. We then moved to an era of Computerization and Data processing. In the following phase, importance of software technology rose, and we had many IT companies creating solutions for BFSI segment, hence there was an emphasis on technical skills, project management skills and skills like Business Analysts, Product Managers, etc.

Now we are in the Fintech era, which is driven by Digital Technology, and here there is an added emphasis on skills related to Community, Partnership, APIs, Regulations, Content, Loyalty, gamification, Data and Analytics, etc. and this is what we have tried to highlight in the emerging roles and career opportunities above. We will also notice that, though each of these are specific roles, they are interdependent, and there is good amount of overlap or shall we say handshake between these roles. This implies that irrespective of the role one plays, they will need to have some level of generalized skills and understanding on most of these aspects, as they are interrelated. This is where 3F – Future Fintech Framework, serves as a building block and bridge between all these roles, providing them with a picture on how they can possibly collaborate with each other across FDLC, FLARE and FAM.

GOING FORWARD

It is important to note that most existing Financial Service businesses are focussed on Products, Processes and Operations. Accordingly, most existing Fintech solutions have been created from this perspective. Going forward, these will increasingly be standardized and be available as API. So, there will be little to differentiate amongst players.

The focus is therefore beginning to shift from Products to Customers. So, aspects like User Experience, Functionality, Engagement, Needs, Usability, etc. will be key for new Fintech solutions, thereby creating the differentiation and offering value to clients.

3F – Future Fintech Framework, precisely enables this shift in focus, from Product to Customer, thereby accelerating Fintech Firms ability to quickly innovate and easily create new solutions. So, lets summarize how this happens:

a. Various themes outlined initially in the book enable us to think of various ways to innovate and differentiate.

b. Fintech Digital Life Cycle (FDLC) enables us to create end to end user journeys, for various products and solutions in Fintech.

c. FLARE provides a logical architecture, which will enable us to assemble a solution as per FDLC.

d. Fintech API Marketplace (FAM) will provide us with the APIs to create FLARE.

e. Various other aspects covered in slight detail like Regulations, player types, changing cost and income paradigms, Emerging roles etc., helps to plan for business, career opportunities and risks.

Trust the above will enable all the readers to become more tuned to the Fintech segment, innovate and be better prepared for growth opportunities going forward.

This book is proposed as a first step towards creating a Future Fintech Framework. We shall keep refining and updating the same and hope to engage with you, and receive your feedback. So, feel free to write to us at futurefintechframework@gmail.com

Let's Accelerate Innovation.

Some Famous Quotes which resonate with 3F – Future Fintech Framework

Sr. No.	Famous Quotes	How It Resonates With 3F
1	"The most powerful person in the world is the storyteller. The storyteller sets the vision, values and agenda of an entire generation that is to come" – Steve Jobs	3F enables you to convert your product into user journeys and stories using FDLC. These journeys can then be realized through FLARE and FAM
2	"You can't connect the dots looking forward; you can only connect them looking backward. So, you have to trust that the dots will somehow connect in your future. You have to trust in something — your gut, destiny, life, karma, whatever…" – Steve Jobs	You can trust and apply 3F to create innovative and futuristic Fintech products and solutions
3	"The more you learn, the more you have a framework that the knowledge fits into." – Bill Gates	3F is one such framework, which presents most aspects about Fintech in a structured form, for you to easily relate and assimilate
4	"You don't have to be a genius or a visionary or even a college graduate to be successful. You just need a framework and a dream" – Micheal Dell	3F gives you such a framework

Sr. No.	Famous Quotes	How It Resonates With 3F
5	"You can't sell anything if you can't tell anything." –Beth Comstock, Vice Chair of General Electric	3F enables you to create an engaging proposition, FDLC is like a customer's journey i.e. Each theme is a story to tell
6	"We're witnessing the creative destruction of financial services, rearranging itself around the consumer. Who does this in the most relevant, exciting way using data and digital, wins!" – Arvind Sankaran	3F is focussed on customers
7	"At the end of the day, customer centric Fintech solutions are going to win." – Giles Sutherland, Carta Worldwide	3F helps you create a customer-centric solution

Source: Internet

www.ingramcontent.com/pod-product-compliance
Lightning Source LLC
Chambersburg PA
CBHW031052180526
45163CB00002BA/799